THE PATTERN MORE COMPLICATED

PHOENIX **POETS**

The Pattern More Complicated

NEW AND SELECTED POEMS

ALAN WILLIAMSON

THE UNIVERSITY OF CHICAGO PRESS
Chicago and London

ALAN WILLIAMSON is professor of English at the University of California, Davis. He is the author of four critical works, most recently *Almost a Girl: Male Writers and Female Identification* (2001), and four books of poems, most recently *Res Publica* (1998), published by the University of Chicago Press.

The University of Chicago Press, Chicago 60637
The University of Chicago Press, Ltd., London
© 2004 by The University of Chicago
All rights reserved. Published 2004
Printed in the United States of America

13 12 11 10 09 08 07 06 05 04   1 2 3 4 5

ISBN: 0-226-89948-9 (cloth)
ISBN: 0-226-89949-7 (paper)

Library of Congress Cataloging-in-Publication Data

Williamson, Alan (Alan Bacher), 1944–
    The pattern more complicated : new and selected poems / Alan Williamson.
       p. cm. — (Phoenix poets)
    ISBN 0-226-89948-9 (cloth : alk. paper) — ISBN 0-226-89949-7 (pbk : alk. paper)
    I. Title. II. Series.

PS3573 .I45623P38 2004
811'.54—dc22

                                                              2003064577

∞ The paper used in this publication meets the minimum requirements of the American National Standard for Information Sciences—Permanence of Paper for Printed Library Materials, ANSI Z39.48-1992.

for Jeanne Foster

The world becomes stranger, the pattern more complicated
Of dead and living.

—T. S. ELIOT, "EAST COKER"

Contents

Acknowledgments • *xiii*

From THE MUSE OF DISTANCE (1988)

Fallings from Us, Vanishings • *3*
The City • *5*
The Chair • *8*
Mr. Brown • *11*
The Muse of Distance • *13*
Small College: All Male: Early 1960s • *29*
From an Airplane • *31*
The Light's Reading • *33*
East Arlington • *36*
Sandy • *38*
Obsession • *41*
The Prayer of the Cathars • *42*
Art Roman • *45*
Recitation for the Dismantling of a Hydrogen Bomb • *47*

From LOVE AND THE SOUL (1995)

Epilogue • *53*
Love and the Soul • *61*
Requited Love • *64*
Fragments: Traveling in Marriage • *76*
Domestic Architecture • *78*
Wide-Angle Shot: Return to Snowy River • *79*
Deb's Dream about Pavese • *80*

Your Forest-Moonlight Picture · 82
Toward the New Year · 83
The Ambivalent Man · 85
Forest Street · 89
Rilke's Argument with Don Giovanni · 91
The Author Reconsiders · 93
Unanticipated Mirrors · 95
Enthusiasm · 99
Highway Restaurant · 100
For My Daughter, Leaving · 102
Tidepools · 104

From RES PUBLICA (1998)

A Childhood Around 1950 · 111
Dreams of Sacrifice · 112
Paint It Black · 115
Listening to Leonard Cohen · 118
After the Election, 1984 · 121
Speakers from the Ice · 122
La Pastorela · 126
Mansard Dreams · 131
Linda Does My Horoscope · 134
Puccini Dying · 138
In Paradiso, speriamo bene · 140
Caitlin: A Biography · 143
Dinosaurs · 145
After "Death of a Porn Queen": Traveling the Great Basin · 148
Red Cloud · 149

From PRESENCE (1983)

Friends Who Have Failed · 157

For Robinson Jeffers · *158*
House-Moving from Tournon to Besançon · *160*
A Progress of the Soul · *165*
For My Grandfather · *168*
Trois Gymnopédies · *169*
If, on Your First Love's Wedding Day · *175*
Dream Without End · *176*
Bernini's Proserpine · *183*
Aubade, Reconstructed in Tranquility · *189*
C., Again · *190*
Spring Trains · *193*
Customs of the Barbarians · *194*
Last Autumn in Charlottesville · *197*
Heaven · *199*
Childless Couple · *201*
Van Gogh's Asylum · *203*
Old Toys Come Back · *205*

New Poems: THE PATTERN MORE COMPLICATED

Theory of Evil · *209*
Adultery · *211*
The Factory · *213*
Where the Hills Come Down Like a Lion's Paw on Summer · *214*
The Cure of Longing · *216*
Martin Sloan · *218*
The Fever of Brother Barnabas · *220*
A Place · *222*
Letter to a Dead Poet · *223*
At the Villa Serbelloni: 1998 · *225*
MLA Notes (1988) · *227*
MLA Notes II (1998) · *229*
The Cost · *231*

· xi ·

Moving Back to Charlottesville · *232*
Villanelle: For Anne · *233*
Autumn Reparations · *234*
The Pattern More Complicated · *235*
Fantasia on some sentences from Combray · *240*
Primrose Hill · *242*
Nostos · *244*

Notes · *247*

Acknowledgments

Poems from the "New" section have appeared in the following magazines:

The American Poetry Review: "Adultery," "The Factory," "Theory of Evil"
Barrow Street: "At the Villa Serbelloni: 1998"
Chicago Review: "The Cost," "The Cure of Longing"
TriQuarterly: "The Fever of Brother Barnabas," "MLA Notes," "MLA Notes II," "The Pattern More Complicated," "Primrose Hill"
The Virginia Quarterly Review: "Where the Hills Come Down Like a Lion's Paw on Summer"
The Yale Review: "Moving Back to Charlottesville," "Nostos"
"Where the Hills Come Down Like a Lion's Paw on Summer" also appeared in *Hammer and Blaze: A Gathering of Contemporary American Poets* (University of Georgia Press, 2002).

*

I would like to thank the Rockefeller Foundation, and the staff of the Villa Serbelloni, for the quiet and detachment needed to begin this rearrangement.

I have been very lucky over the years in my initial readers, who have often made poems better than I would ever have made them left entirely to myself. I would like to mention in particular Debra Allbery, Frank Bidart, Paul Breslin, Jeanne Foster, my teacher Robert Lowell, James McMichael, Robert Pinsky, Richard Tillinghast, Richard Wertime, Anne Winters, my daughter Elizabeth, and the poetry group in Berkeley including Chana Bloch, Sandra Gilbert, Diana O'Hehir, Peter Dale Scott, and Phyllis Stowell.

from **THE MUSE OF DISTANCE (1988)**

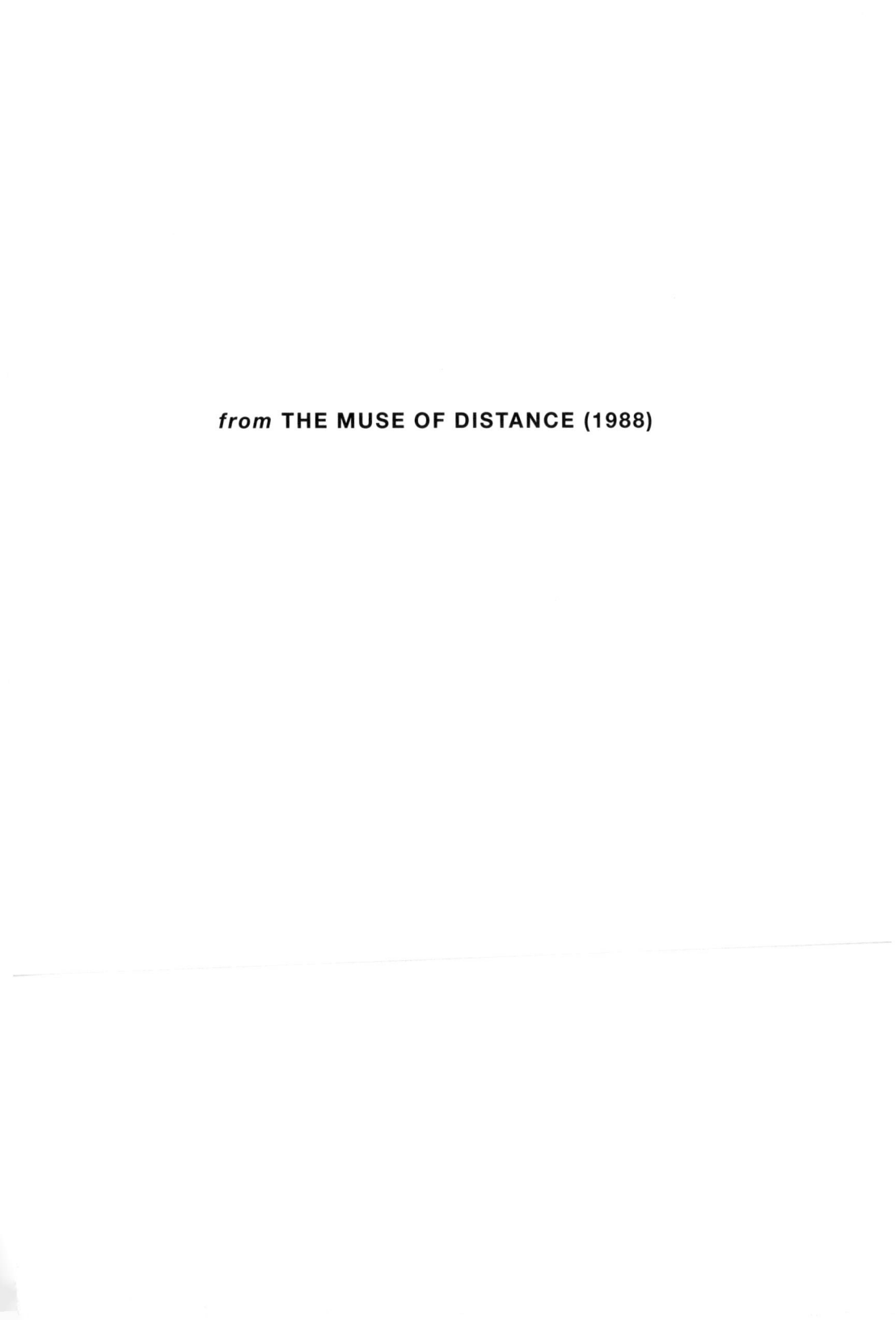

Fallings from Us, Vanishings

Sometimes you came home from the beach with a wasp-sting, or
a speck of sand that even the eye-cup wouldn't wash out.
The day was troublingly larger for being spent
empty, among bodies—as if some great purpose
had been found or missed, looking out to the stationary
water-intake boat, the *crib* (did anyone live there?).
And when you got home, and the sun stayed insidiously
involved in your skin, all indoors seemed delicious
and temporary, like a glass of water.

Or in the early autumn dark, when you came out of
a movie theater, and something cruel, from another world—
the plague; a slave crushed dragging a stone for the Pyramids—
stayed with you, you were afraid to go out to the end
of the long hall, where the small one crooked off to the bathroom,
sensing it, and you, would shelve off into another
space you could feel, though you couldn't know or explain . . .

And it was almost a relief to carry the telescope down
and set its metal legs with a small crisp tinkle
on the playground asphalt (the city stood around silent
like its cardboard skyline in the planetarium).
And then the slight shock of floating out through your eye
to those bodies of gas and nothing, the Coal-Sack Nebula,
across the clean, unlivable, untraversable years.

It made you imagine the world was God's body, split
from some first atom, that was neither world nor God.
You wrote about that for school—"accounts of Creation"—
then refused to read it aloud, because no one else's
was like it, the boys' all science, the girls' all Biblical.
But while you thought about it outdoors, the dangerous night
held its distance; or if not, you could hear it far off, coming
with the same slight ping over the wintry ground.

The City

—A kind of map of the mind, or of life . . .

Eastward, in the fragile curtain we lived in,
all brilliance, tracery, flutings, the mind's feminine
enchantment with itself—crystalline rooms—
it blows against the Lake,

                  light out of darkness,
as the long parks at its feet, abandoned now
to monstrosity, for those hours,
tell you by night; as the gloomy, steeped and over-steeped
last oak leaf of its brick tells you by day.

(One night, a man in one of those towers saw
a shadow detach from the tree-shadow and steal after
a woman, oblivious, in the sulphur brilliance
of the arc lights. She was dead when he put down the phone.)

Then the space behind, with nothing to stop it—beginning
in the loneliness of certain upper
office stories, hundreds of snowy doors,
in the buildings downtown; hurled westward on the El's
black interruption of the air of Gilded
Age shopping streets, to the neighborhoods where life
grew violent and thin with reduplication,
like the great letters stencilled in a fungus

of end-of-winter lavender, char-black, rose,
on the walls where the ads have passed.

Somehow I never felt the invisible country
as ending it (notwithstanding the bits
of green at the moraine rise, distant banners
in summer's heavier, wavy industrial air)—

any more than the Lake, with its visible, invisible
far shore, ended anything.

                        If there was culmination
near the shales of the beaches, in the blankness
of late November, it was those eyes opening
on endlessness, the museums:
                                 out past the small airfield,
spun silk of comets dream-depthless in the slightly
brown far space of early
observatory plates; or the glowing ring
of the Table of the Elements, rounded warily
for fear of the whistle from the reconstructed
coal mine grazing the dome beyond.

                               It was in an under-
ground lecture chamber there, all muralless blank tan
plaster, I heard of *The Birth*
and Death of the Sun; the earth made uninhabitable
in the last explosions.
                       That I and everyone
I knew would be dead, didn't help. My friend thought we would have colonized
other solar systems by then. I pinned my hopes
on a race of people who had learned to travel
at the speed of the earth's turning, living constantly

westward, on the cusp of the sun's rising,
in a new kind of car that hovered inches
above deserts and oceans; sometimes gaining an hour
or two of night, to sleep in something still
not fire-twisted beyond use; some thing like the Field Museum's
caveman's cave . . .

The Chair

The ten years I've owned it, unapproachable:

Shaker-square; its bottom a cage; its seat
tight-woven, tobacco- and pale-cornhusk-speckly
as an old man's hand, with almost no give from the years
it gave you comfort, the window behind, light falling
from the desk lamp; on the wall, the bitten-in iron wrinkles
of King Charles and John Dryden . . . It was where you lived,
except for the long planetary loops
through the apartment, your face appearing, eager,
at my reluctantly open adolescent door.

Once a famous man, who revered you,
described your first class of the term. You were having a controversy
with another scholar. You came in, laid your green Harvard bookbag
down, took out a book and stared straight into it
until you sensed the students were all
assembled; then looked up and began, "Now *he* says . . ."

Too often, too early, I was the "he" that said
something that could not be swallowed, or let pass.
A thousand miles away, I've had to follow
the endless, cornered turnings of your hurt
reasoning—the chair, the stillness, the long hall—
like a chess partner, unable to withdraw
my attention, because you could not withdraw yours,

day after day, hour after hour . . .
I cannot sit in it to think or write.

Yet how hard you tried to escape from it, the years after
your first illness, when I was twelve—
to enjoy without doing: listening for an hour,
after lunch, to your records of the new, sad, witty
French music, *Les Six*—though really almost preferring
to search out newer ones in the catalogues . . .

Or how we "broke in" our new Ford
each bright fall weekend, driving north
in the white sickle of the autumn light
and your easily angered travel-nerves, to Yerkes
Observatory—prism of leaves downhill
to the cold lake—or the bratwurst restaurant
you remembered, in Milwaukee, from before I was born.

And after, returning, caught on the expressway
in the choke of early dark, moving with the other
accidental cars—the seamed tired faces, children
restless in back, in blue—
                                     I thought of the
empty apartments they moved to scattering leaflike
as their presence beside us in the night, one slipping
ahead, one returned by magic as our lane
slid forward. And back at last, heating our makeshift
meal out of cans, it took a while for the glaze
of home to settle again onto our own
echoing cavern, brown Braques and Légers.

I wanted us so to be happy and at ease,
and we were, halfway; so something clings

about our objects, still crying out
for something more to be done with them, and yet nothing
that is not betokened in the calm and stillness
of their deep shine.
                      And the chair, where once
I hid in the under-cage and watched the sun
whiten the dust-motes . . . As I grow older, it seems
to go on getting smaller: when I am dead,
I can imagine it no longer human-
scale, still perfectly polished, in some museum
of styles or souls—strange ones, tied to their places
as a child to his cradle or a martyr to
his tongs . . .
                 In their bright shirts, without ties,
the new easy people pass our cage and comment
on the turn of the century; Protestantism; the grimness
of Swedes; the fastidiousness
and guilt of those who rise
above their origins; the long winter of the Great Plains . . .
I am always half gone on with them and half
held back by my need to argue with,
convince, demolish, do justice to and shield
and rescue you—cage and prisoner,
but, while I live, never not the scale of life.

Mr. Brown

He came from a small town in downstate Illinois,
and couldn't believe it when his city students
laughed at the notion that you could hear the corn grow
on soft summer nights. He got me to eat
a fried grasshopper once. His chuckle came low and bland
from inside his sheath of baby fat; his eyelids
were neatly, symmetrically pursed, like the valves of a clam.

Between assurances that our easily sliced-up
flatworm, named Elvis,
would regenerate in days, he was the class
matchmaker. He gave us shyer ones lists of girls
to ask to the Prom; and then—as no adult
had ever spoken to me—"Who knows? You might
give it all up, get married, go and work
in the steel mills. That's the power of your chemistry.
I mean the chemistry of your body, of course."

No date that time. But later, the thought of smokestacks
in South Chicago, across the dreamlike gulf
from the school towers,
helped bridge the other gulf when Karen, dancing,
said in her sensible voice, "Hold me closer,"
as if it were no more than Mr. Brown showing me
a firmer way to shake hands . . .

When the jocks started saying, "Brown's a homo"
in the locker room, I thought with stricken loyalty,
if he is, I must be too; then when he crooked a finger
under my belt buckle, talking in the hall,
a holy dread . . .
                till tamed by absence, though never listed
matter-of-factly among "gay" friends, he stood,
a kind of Terminus, or excluded Moses, over
the long descent to where we are ropes, ribbons
bird shrill electric outlets dizziness
like the first seawater's, waking to its own presence
somehow jelled from the sun . . .

The Muse of Distance

What composes a life? Mine comes, too much, from books;
but also the sense that, if you climbed high places,

you would see the streets go on with nothing to end them,
and be driven to, perhaps even desire,

whatever they withheld: a flight of smokestacks past water;
a girl in a mean, dawn-blue room; a glimpse of the terrible

engines, or giants, it took to make such a world . . .

*

Far in the caverns of our night, a jarring:
then chinks of light

at both doors to my room, and sausage-smells from our huge
travellers' breakfast; then lugging the suitcases, down

from the hiding-places where they'd kept all winter—
tribal ochre: the trademark an Indian's head

off an old penny—down the long stairwell, black
rail, white balusters, to the mirroring black-

and-white tile at the foot, not scarily dim now, but bathed
through the jewel-faceted panes

of the entrance hall beyond, in silveriness
without origin or ray . . .   So our years came round, as far back

as I can remember, to this ritual of detaching
ourselves from ourselves westward:

our summer in California; half the continent's
breadth; a journey reliving

my father's childhood, failure by fresh start, westward;
which was, perhaps, why his nerves flared to get away

at seven, on schedule, so that he lashed out at
my mother or me, some wrong way I packed the trunk

or failed to make it lock—"If you grew up
the way most people do, that's what your precious

intelligence would be judged by!"—betraying not only
me, but his whole life there, with the quiet,

the high-ranged books . . . And yet the happiness,
the *Nunc Dimittis*, when we set our course down

the east-west numbered streets, half-fused with the sun risen
from the lake behind us, touching with unwitnessing strangeness

—as, back in the apartment, I had touched
the dinosaur bones on my dresser, knowing nothing

would change their position or how the light would pass them
all the days till fall—the dewy Gothic mirage

of the University; the Negro blocks; the airport's
prairie-tan lanes . . .

When we passed the garbage dump, my father marvelled
in hoots and youks, and held his nose, as if everything

he hated in his life were exposed, concentrated,
rotted and burned at once. For the next half hour—

the country coming on, meadowlarks starting
from the wet ditchgrass, but the great heat rising

more unimpeded than ever in the city—
he sang:

> *You were my girl in cal-i-co,*
> *I was your bashful barefoot beau,*
> *I wrote on your slate, I love you so,*
> *When we were—a couple—of kids!*

*

My Great-Uncle George hopped the train where it slowed
for the curve near the family farm
eight miles out of Galesburg. He'd done it often,
but this January night couldn't awaken
conductor or passengers. I can imagine
the corridor through the window, lucid, empty,
and how he managed, in the gathering speed, to unbuckle
and reloop his belt around some grip.

                         They found his
frozen body still hanging there in the gaslight
of the Chicago yards.

                    I imagine my father
was named for him, whether before or after
I've no idea. In any case, they moved West
so early and repeatedly, the death
could only have followed like a kind of legend
or coat-of-arms.
                    Often, crossing the Midwest,
on the new bypass skirting some blind place-name,
my father would say, "I went to high school here,"
or "we had a farm," and then "only my poor father
would have bought such land. I suppose they bailed him
out. They always did."

                    We never stopped to visit
those family places, though once we were turned away
at the Brown Palace dining room in Denver, because
I had no tie on. (I was fourteen.)
"Take a look anyway," my father said shyly,
and nudged me past a door—the wrought-iron well
above the lobby, leather sofas: "That's where
I sat and held the gold brick!"
                         —a real one;
for maybe half an hour, while Uncle Alvin
went upstairs and made his calls.

Next morning we drove out an indeterminate, elm-lined boulevard
to a lavender-Gothic house. When I got out
to take a picture, he said I was "making a spectacle";

and then, as we pulled away, "it must have been here
that I had the t.b. That bilious attic room."

And I said, "It *must?* But Daddy, don't you know?"

Then off again: but that night I wondered
just what he was revisiting when, as often,
he groaned himself to sleep.
                              (Though my mother once
returned from the thin-walled motel bathroom, her voice
a mixture of panic and triumph—"They were saying,
*'do you think there's something wrong
with that man in there?'* "
                              —it was not an
unmusical sound: long, falling, half a sigh,
like wind in the wires, or a train distancing.)

*

But what I remember best are the anonymous towns
whose Main Streets we walked at twilight, drugged
with the slow lift of six-hundred-mile days
—not even stared at: as though our speed were written
like a protective mark, across our brows—
in those Main Streets still smelling of grass, or the desert's sharpness . . .

It was the things that wrenched at me the most
in those places: a dead firm's name still silver-dollared
in the cool pavement between new display windows;
and all the tools, that lived and toughened and rusted with
men's hands—the unsold harvesters shining
in the first fall light, more terrible than the graveyards
one passed on the outskirts, Indian-fringed with alders . . .

The things were like a song, that could only be heard near the earth,
only two or three inches above it: of men becoming
what they did to live; of raw skill, contempt for the mind;
or just of conditions, equal and without rancor,
of the slow flesh, that has no hope not to vanish
with all it touches . . . whispering, near the earth.

And yet if it was high summer, and the road wound
along the bluffs where the tall old scalloped houses
stood embraced by verandas, I invariably
would ask my mother, "Don't you wish we lived here?"
She would sigh, or else be drawn—*of course not, no
theater, no art museums, no real friends*—

And she was right: I didn't, really; what I loved
were the Triple A timetable cards, *Vandalia
16 minutes, 30 minutes Centralia;*
the never quite being in one place, the wind
always the same through the scarcely opened windows;

and yet being everywhere; and, as I grew older, imagining
someone waiting—as if I were called to scatter love
like a wanderer scattering apples, through death's arbitrary
stations and ends . . .

*

—When the moon moves and the bare driftwood splinters
stand out on the Nevada station wall
I close my eyes, lie on a hard bench, and see
when I am too guilty to picture you, it is you,
the scarps toward your breasts . . .

—It is last year's antlers, pointing somewhere in the mountains.

—Yes, you were always one for pointing elsewhere;
and yet there is no place you have not given.
You always lived in the only house with a tower
in the level prairie town.
Your hair was the red Southern clearing, its snakes and lianas;
your eyes a torn screen door
somewhere flashing on coolness.
The empty watery taste of motel air at day's end
is a scarf
you left behind you,
a view of weeds in new earth by a train scar.

And when we meet at the last cottonwood
going into the desert,
drawn up in the dry whisper
of her leaves on themselves
over and over,
will we spring together
into the final jewelcase of the air?

—We are lying together so far across the moonlight,
you can feel the weeds start growing through your hair.

*

Aunt Mary Alice always asked if the girls I liked
had auburn hair. Uncle Harold, she said, always
liked auburn-haired girls—
                      though hers was dark, darker
than the foxfur stole I loved on her, with the real

little teeth and paws, and the little tawny depthless
glass-chip eyes.

     —This was beyond the desert,
beyond the distance where America
almost floats off in the blueness between mesas
and thunderheads, an opaline shudder neither
transparence nor obstruction . . .
         beyond that end, a city
that seemed a slightly seasick form of motion,
sea palms and mountain pines, the smell of driving,
the center always just behind you—unless

it centered, as for me, up stairs exhaling
dry stucco, in a room with carefully kept
American coin silver, the mantel clock bonging,
and a sampler with not HOME SWEET HOME but a woolly
locomotive, car, and ocean liner, and OVER
THE LAND / OVER THE SEA / TRAVELLING FAR AND WIDE.

And under it, leg raised and gauzed, no traveller
but a man cars couldn't keep from leaping onto—
off of jacks; unnoticed and unbraked in driveways—
until he had little underarm skin left to be grafted
and "take," or not, over long weeks, on his leg's
reopened tread,
    my Uncle Harold sat waiting,
eyes bulging as he talked, a rapid-fire
high harmonica twang of hyperbolic
bewilderment, that comes back a tune without words, or the broken
words of old age: how his footsteps cracked in the air
of subzero prairie mornings; how they drove a hundred miles
to pick up everyone, "out to Burbank, the big bands came there—"

A song heard near the earth, only two or three inches above it . . .

And my father listening, almost abashed, only later
shaking his head at how much he'd heard about fishing trips—
yet fond, and almost guilty; and, for all his professorial
moustache, so like his brother, their long skulls
all angles and knobs, and the hair spurting out of them
in short sparky wires—all hardness, but hardness never
at peace with itself: the expression formal, shy,
and ready to break apart in *Jeepers creepers*
haywire whimsy—like a machine some Futurist
was designing, while they walked to school, on the icy Plains.

*

What held him there in L.A.?—the mantel clock bonging
musically, with a long premonitory rasp
on the quarter hour, that, hurrying time, held it
still, unimportant, adrift . . .

                    My grandfather,
in the Depression—the last farm gone, the cow
sold, it was said, "so George could go to college"—
failed to see a streetcar as he came home one sunrise
from his last job, night-watchman
at a warehouse, in L.A. . . .

                    And all his children
lingered, except my father, already gone; and one
uncle, whom I hardly knew,
retired early, married late, and bought a trailer,
and lived, it seemed, in a kind of roving family
of trailer-couples, linking up near Christmas

in Guadalajara; in the spring, up Oregon way . . .

depthless, to us, as if he'd stepped off in that air
between mesa and cloud.

*

I thought I knew what Uncle Harold did. Then, once, at our place
(our summer place, in Monterey) a wall-outlet failed.

I said, "We'll have to get an electrician."
Uncle Harold said, "I am an electrician."

I said, "You're kidding. I thought you—"
                                        and suddenly
I didn't quite know what I'd thought. I looked to my father,
but he just looked surprised, and said with an indefinable
hurt in his voice,
            "Of course your Uncle Harold
is an electrician."

Harold worked for Lockheed: the intricate
circuits that held the big jets up in the sky.
But that wasn't the point: my mother and I were outsiders
on any such ground.
                    Sometimes, on the trip, he'd compare
his arm with ours, where it rested, freckle-stained
as a gas station floor, on the rim of the open window—
"I can't tan the way you people do, I only burn";
or watching a home movie, after twenty years, would get angry
at the way she was standing, off by herself, in the hallway
of his parents' house.
                    And one winter, in Chicago—

"I'm not going to work in the factory, after all,"
I yelled at him.

(I'd gotten a D in Phys. Ed. For two weeks, total silence
on the subject. I conferred with my mother:

"But those aren't his values. He doesn't play ball, or—"

And she: "Whatever men want for themselves, for their sons
they want the other."
                        "But a professor—"

                               "Just
because they're professors, they can't stop being men . . ."

—leaving me wondering just what *I* was, included
in this sad, superior, helpless, womanly
understanding . . .)

            Now, *going to work in the factory*
hung in the lunch-table air. Then my father saying,
with deadly calm,
            "Two of my brothers did."

I rushing in heedless, "But Daddy, you were the exception
in your family. If a professor's kid—"

He managed the worldly, world-weary smile of his prose,
feeling fused with intellect. "Oh, I know,
you're the exception—"

"I didn't say that. What I said was, *you* were—"

Then the voice of the Lord in thunder, drowning me out:

"You're the exception! You're always the exception!"

*

Two of my brothers did: it was his wish
he hated, completed in mine.

                      When Uncle Harold
failed to show up for a family reunion, or awkwardly
we had to shift at the last minute and stay
with one of my aunts—
                      As a child, I didn't notice.
Later, the explanations:

                "He can't touch a drop now, or—"

"He was the one who went down to the morgue when our father—"

But Aunt Mary Alice, looking down at her own
arthritis-jewelled fingers,
said once, "Harold has fine hands, a surgeon's hands.
He wanted to be a doctor, but the Depression—
and 'the cow was sold for George to go to college'—"

When I told my father, he winced, as if he'd bitten
something sour, then sighed, "Harold wanted to be everything.
He was going to write a great novel, and we'd all
be famous from it. He'd make a million dollars
on the movie—"

He didn't, of course. Like my father, he gave

half his paycheck to keep their parents in their own house,
until the sunrise and the streetcar . . .

He *did his duty*, in that brontosaurian
language my father spoke more, when they'd been together,
as he laughed at jokes on "the colored"; remembered his Model T Ford.

*

When "the t.b." returned in him, after years
of late-night writing, slowly angrier nerves,
and he hung in the balance all summer, needing seven
times the normal dose of drugs
                             —small wonder
I turned to Christ, the eternal
son, who dies a little
(or much) to live beyond his father's justice
without calling it a lie.

              I gave up my childhood anger—
its study of execution and torture, that put the iron
and smoke of Chicago winter into my soul—
in a kind of floating calm, a long June
dusk of forgiveness, in which the city
lay murmuring interfused, the dying
and the newly born.

              I thought it ungodly to fear death;
though in daydreams I saw my spirit, airborne
above my body, in a hospital bed like my father's,
hover near the bowed heads, ecstatic to tell them how silly
they were not to know how simple it was—then pausing
in a white ceiling corner, not quite sure where to go.

And my father, in his loose-hanging hospital gown,
haggard, slowed down enough to be sweet and wry,
not embarrassed, at my first crush on a girl—
making me know the Mystery
was simply true: in suffering, we were reborn.

But, when he recovered, things weren't much changed. He'd still
sing, as on leaving Chicago, the last ten miles
approaching "our shanty." But when we'd actually driven
up Monterey Heights, almost to its scalplock of pines . . .

It's a scene I somehow never entirely escape from.
The fog already coming in; or perhaps not, and glare.
The earthless white granite soil and pine-needle duff.
My parents go over every inch of the house
for "the tenants' " misdoings, every vanished glass or
scratch in the varnish, as if it would tell them what
is missing from what they wanted.

                                            Wherever they move, the floor gives
its slight, incurable booming reverberation
from the space too big for a crawl-space and never
finished as a cellar. My father's anger mounts,
shakes everything, ceases, each year, in no particular
proportion to what is lost.

                                    I sit in my room, too visible
from the other rooms, the stucco arc of street;
and as I might think of a person—a pair of perfect,
calm, understanding eyes—think of Chicago,
where there are other people, worn gold
interiors to glimpse from the car at night, returning,
in a rush of such black, such deep-gripped-down

cottonwood trees, my own life would grip down
and sleep on itself, dark, full, opening our door
on rich books, peaceful must.

                        But that is gone
to the far side of the summer. Christ
is less a refuge. If I am not to live
a frozen ghost in the middle wind, a distance
that can never become a place, I must

be here, with them.

                      *

When I was fourteen I made up a sentence: *we are unhappy
because we have no roots.*
I wasn't sure of it; I'd read something like it in *Time*.
Perhaps we weren't unhappy, or *too many roots*
would have been truer . . .

                      But I know it struck on
something in me; some place where I was dreaming,
against us, an image of the true house, solid
on the solid land: the summers falling stationary
through the bay windows; piano music dampered
at night, in the thick leaves; and up the stairs
unnumbered branching alcoves, sisters, silences—

like a house in a book, where a distant lake was visible
from one upper window—enough endlessness
to rest a family in each other and
the ground beneath,
                    so that, if one lived there, a life

would fall like an image: first love to white stone a falling
of original leaves . . .
                        and the unseen sister upstairs
comes out and gathers it all into her hands.

That was my dream, as we passed the small towns sleeping . . .
But what my father remembered (though he could never approve of himself
for having arrived there) were the intimations
of a world beyond: how a store would have, from some wanderer,
almost postage-stamp-sized books, *The Ballad of Reading Gaol* or
Non Sum Qualis Eram Bonae Sub Regno Cynarae . . .

And though I said *we are unhappy, we have no roots,* I know
when I reach back as far as I can for an image
of happiness, I come to images of travel:

the DIP signs in the desert, the runningboards
and buck-tan interiors of '40s cars;
or asking my parents, in Needles, California,
one night when I was four, "How far away are the stars?"—

expecting I don't know what, a few city blocks
or even as far as L.A.—and then the vastness
of the answer somehow soothing, as our departure
soothed, back in Chicago, the dinosaur bones, the chairs . . .

We seem contented in vastness, as we do not, wholly,
anyplace solid, where our weight and distance
can be determined . . . in this, "the exception"
though we are forever, most purely American.

Small College: All Male: Early 1960s

The boys who would never admit they miss their mothers
hate the dietician. When she walks past the tables, at night,
The food eats shit—The food eats shit—they sing—
Hi-ho the dairy-oh the food eats shit. God,
there's little to be proud of there; except that one was not, in one's turmoil,
quite as blind as Bernie, who changed his name to B. Dov,

allowing the dining-hall announcer to read, "Beat-off
Lederberg will show his films *Moth-err*
and *Hand-Heat*"—spoon banging, turmoil,
and Bernie: "Read it right, asshole"—"in the Common Room tonight."
And all that freshman talk about sex and God,
the machines we were caught in!—while the late-night hissing

of the radiators gave way to the long sing-
ing sweep of wind up our hill; or rain, far off.
"We are being pissed on from the prick of God,"
my roommate said. And I thought how they—the fathers and mothers—
wouldn't understand, not seeing how cosmic Night
loomed on us, and the gallantry of our turmoil.

I don't feel any easier now about that turmoil,
or surer what part of it still sings.
Nothing rubs the deeper blackness from those nights.
It was one thing to talk all the time about "beating off,"

another to push a door, not meant to give, and (*mother-
fucking lock!*) a friend's hand, nailed to its terrible god.

I thought my Christian friend was looking for God,
when he walked out into the snowstorm, that spoke to his turmoil
like Oedipus vanishing into the gorge of the Mothers.
But what tormented him was another singing,
and the whiteness so electric—he couldn't just beat off—
but had to walk, imagine glances, risk knives, all the city's night.

Was that the night I realized how our night
was full of music, like an island full of gods?
Only say that you'll be mine—someone's banjo off
somewhere—*And in our home*—*happy*—that turmoil—
Down beside where the waters flow—and mix and sing
(in whose room, on what floor?) the future, the murder, the mother.

It seems a kind of off-key voice of God,
that singing always somewhere, under the night,
motherly, lonely; repeating and changing our turmoil.

From an Airplane

From an airplane the two valley towns seem equal
to each other, along the axis of the mountains,
though the only road between snakes twenty—thirty?—
miles to the north, where narrowing canyons open
the possibility.
                You hold the two
in your eye as in God's hand, the same statistical
print-out of roofs, gone blank with snow; and think
how if you lived there you would love, hate, marry
someone in the next five houses; perhaps never
get as far as the mirror-town, before you died;
or if you started to walk there, how measuredly the cold
would rise in your boots with the first, the second field.

Where you'll land, it's just less visible. In the many
streets and cubicles, someone, just separated,
feels the dead years in his furniture as a measure
like cold in his bootsoles; or he turns back, stays married,
and the unlived town stays in the empty balance . . .
But the restaurants hide it more, the headlines, the friends.

On the whole you'd rather be up here forever,
where the fact that the earth curves is actually visible,
blued with its unexperienceable other time;
not come down at all—unless, of course, you could live

like the Acoma people, stunned for centuries
with the sense of being at the center.
            It could absorb
anything, even the Cross: they carried beams
thirty miles on their shoulders from Mount Taylor
and any that touched the ground couldn't be used
in the church roof; they were tapered
to candy-cane-colored "candles" for the reredos.
The bells are male and female, because four boys
and four girls were traded to Mexico City for them.
In the pottery, one is always at the center
of interlocking weather—sweeps and stairways
of black, with the little triangles inside them
meaning lightning. It's one of
the thinnest potteries in the world. The ingredients
come from the four directions: north for blackness,
south for white slip, east for yellow slip, west for clay.

The Light's Reading

(Meditations on Edward Hopper)

1
On Sundays, from upstairs, a grown man's voice:
"I love it I love it I love it I love it Yay
Patriots!"
             What do they love? Or the women's spooky
enjoyment of pity: "Isn't that the way . . ."

A man's voice falling, in a hotel corridor, "Yes,
dear, I'm going . . ."

                    Everywhere we fail
to snatch it back off the mirror, this endless falling
of life that only
lives to keep itself going: impenetrable scrim . . .

2
The light's reading of us: by definition, ending
where it begins, like a clockface . . . at times
endlessly fertile and opening—the sun
presses the girl's crisp summer dress back like wind
where she waits at the hot curb,
and you feel behind her every hoarded coolness
of the dim apartments.

>   But always, come August,
the shadows are folded away; then something happens
in the color of the sky, like a trumpet, calling
to the bronze in things: the leaves, the purple horsetails
of the marshgrass, the crazy shingled houses.

Then the fattish girl comes out in her bikini
to sun, once more, on the rail of the upstairs porch,
her mother knitting behind . . .

It is all in her silly, hopeful look out against
where the painting looks: evening blue
distilled in the roofs; the empty room behind her,
where the sun's rim only reaches the white border
of the picture on the wall; and all the mother is keeping
herself from saying . . .

>   the light, like a reader, in love with fate.

3
The man sleeps, his back a shell. The woman, able to bear more—
if only to bear how much they have desired
each wide-pored, graying other—
>   is sitting up.

He seems to float among monoliths: the walls
thickened with what—mere dusk, a hidden airshaft,
closets, plumbing?—

One sees past every wall to another window.

Inexplicable fear of falling: the ringed horizon,
the eternal smokestacks—

So desire towers, and, towering, holds us
over what is beyond any
object: the empty clockface, the rims of time.

4
A man who loves only one woman in his life
empties the space around him with rejected
dreams.
       It is the shock of their going opens
the air as far as death. The people there
look strange, in that long light: at first, more rigid
than the damned in hell; then the rays find a richness
of old metal in the wrinkles, a smile in the sag of the breast—
shimmer of the impenetrable, the pure cells . . .

Was this love, or simply knowledge of the planet
of his cropped head, what life it would bear?—that kept
the picture from filling
with young girls or children, only these two
comedians, the pancake stiff on their faces,
the smiles stiffly waiting to say good-bye . . .

Yet how delicately he paints her vanishing
to him, at the moment when she stands most lovably
still before life. The sky
is behind her wholly. The frame does not let one follow
her arm even as far as the flex to move
her paintbrush. Her look is gone
into whatever has caught it, leaving only
a sidelong spill of light off the lens of the eye.

East Arlington

I stopped there, ten years back, to check a tire,
heading South and home. It stayed with me—an evil
stretch of road, hemmed in by cyclone fences
and cinder shoulders, the town below and hidden
to one side, the other side industrial marshes.
No mechanic on hand. They added air. Behind time,
I didn't care to think the tire might blow
hours later and send three cars balleting
across the Connecticut Turnpike, with, miraculously,
no injuries.   Or to think my life could grow
so accident-thrown that for two years I'd live there,
on a street of shingle and shadowless-siding houses,
so uniform, one spotted the odd half-window
at an upper landing, in time, as eagerly
as an angel hidden, for God's eyes alone,
in a French cathedral.

    But there was a field behind the houses,
an urban field, part marshland in most seasons.
It curved up like the earth to get away from
its horizon of disused tracks and sickly willows,
and the clouds raced across it like the ghosts of the trains.
The city let anyone who wanted to have
an allotment there. Ours was out on the end
and had to be reclaimed, it seemed a foot an hour,

from a turf all roots, bricks, nails, and real New England
granite shards. But it grew beautiful
enough for the twist-mouthed corner toughs to want to
scream through at midnight, at the end of summer,
bending the Portuguese family's iron fences
to curlicues, pulling even the stubborn
eggplants up by the roots.
                            We discovered it at twilight
the following day. All the Sunday gardeners
were standing about; I met a colleague, another
temporary lecturer, I'd always assumed was
some well-off plumber, or office manager.
The police said they knew who'd done it but couldn't move
without an eye-witness.
                        Though my wife and I
had quarreled that day, she said
she couldn't believe my courage when I tamped
the few only-half-uprooted flowers back in,
feeling as I did so how cold the earth
had already gotten, the first killing frost
waiting inches under. But I felt no courage:
a grim, childish tenderness; the one way I had
of mocking evil, or placing my hope in hope.

Sandy

(Virginia; 1970s)

1
At first it's enough just to carry the little gun
to the supermarket—first in one pocket, then
in another. He enjoys the anxiety
of checking for bulges in the shoplifters' mirror.
It gives the aisles an expectancy, a glisten.
He finds he loses his hatred of the women—
the old ones stalled for an hour
in front of a bank of cans, the slightly younger
mowing you down with their carts and pirate smiles.
He learns to allow his eyes to stare.

Strangely, he finds it is often the young mothers
who go most nearly nude there,
bare-bellied under flimsy halters
as the babies who reach up . . .
He is astonished that they can get so angry, and scream so,
way out on the calm white beaches of themselves.

2
He has always wanted to do it in strange
half-abandoned public places: say, a storefront
at midnight, among mannequins, a far spotlight sliding
its sad old-rose refrain across the plaster . . .
Or this: one Sunday, he finds an abandoned quarry
on a dirt road under the mountains,
cliffs of pale dust and sun; a ring of pines.

There is a worn wooden chute in it, leading up
to a kind of house, on stilts,
machinery shadowed through the sieve-like siding.
He would like to climb there, but the underpinnings
go crazy at his weight.
                        He jumps free in terror, then
goes back to test with his hand; and suddenly
feels his skin cling to the dead silvery surface
in which there is something perfect, something that gives joy
in whorls and waves and does not know what it has
to be joyful about: a transparent house, full of pulleys.

3
At last it is only a question of: this day,
or the next, the next? He stands on the softening asphalt,
hoping the eyes of the colored cart-boy pass
over him easily. Does he choose
by ugliness or beauty: the mocking smile held too long
with no one around to mock, or the glassy sheen
of a summer day on an olive collarbone?

He is at the car window, has shown
the gun; it is over. In a different world
he makes her point the car at the wavering mountains.
She will have to undress in the center, so the light
and dust off the cliffs will glitter on her wholly,
as if a small lake appeared there, to dive in . . .
He has almost forgotten the gun; he dandles
it and vague memories of a magician's wand
across his lap.
                He says, "My friends call me Sandy."

Obsession

(After Rodin)

Buried, unformed: the head down in the knee's
undented space, as if it too were skin
merely, to prickle at hot and cold, not measure
any shape beyond it. All that has detail is what
is left unfinished: the quarry-rock of hair
that, over the blank spheroid, makes the cup
of an acorn, down to the slight, vestigial stem . . .
It is the thought that has held her so many months
gelled, opaque, unspeakable; to wait
in blind hope that soon—
leaving scarcely a mark, in the twinkling of an eye—
it will slip from the peculiar, perfect egg, and all
that was inside will be spelled out, root into leaf.

The Prayer of the Cathars

As little known of them as whether they
actually shared their wives, or on the contrary
prescribed deer-hunting to those incapable
of absolute continence, holding it
a lesser gash in the eternal body . . .

> *For the sake of the good He gives*
> *life to the evil, and will do so*
> *as long as there are any of my little ones in the world*

It is known they could live with Jews, Moslems,
and even Christians; that where the four
touched, the Kabbalah,
the cult of Mary, and Western poetry
sprang up in a hundred years.

For whatever endless reasons
they displeased the world; an army moved south
as we've seen armies move—the jeep's
radio antenna lowered playfully
to catch the old man bicycling downhill
at just the right height and snap
his neck.   The propagandists, as always,
spoke of it not as something

anyone did by will, but fire
from heaven, the eagle of Zeus, *Anangke*.

> *And the devil was very false,*
> *for he said that God deceived them*
> *in allowing them to do Good only;*
> *and that he would give them wives they would love greatly;*
> *and he gave them commandment over one another,*
> *so that some should be kings, emperors, and counts,*
> *and that with one bird they might catch another bird,*
> *with one beast, another beast.*

If you were a nobleman you had the right
to be beheaded. But they
could choose to cut your arms and legs off
first.
          Commoners, of course, went to the fire.

                      *

> *Can vei la lauzeta mover* . . .

The song begins: the countertenor voice
rising for the moment when
the sun's first ray transfixes it, and joy
gone to the heart it falls, forgets itself—
forgets, the voice says, its own sex, even the earth—
as, it may be, the Perfect forgot
when they filed down from solar Montségur to die . . .

For the Lady, too, is a mirror from before Nature
looking on whom the self finds the deep sigh

that kills it: lost *com perdet se*
lo bels Narcisus en la fon.

White walls with stammering saints, turned to white bodies.
Nothing survives; or everything
in the shape of its opposite. Their burnt page left
a curve, a bottomlessness
in Europe's certainties—
        even
the navel and winding Salome's veil of Isaiah's
dance at Souillac—
though for two hundred years the churches
were built with arrow-slits at the crenellations.

 And so they rose upon a heaven of glass,
 and as many as elevated themselves there,
 so many fell and perished;
 but God descended with 12 apostles
 and darkened himself in St. Mary.

Art Roman

(Autun, December; Poitou-Charente, July)

The angel wakes us to the star an inch
beyond our heads,
where we sleep, even if we are kings, all under
one cloak . . .

As from the Romans wish to close a gate
on the forest night, *oppidum*
                        —we skidded down
the ice-slick hill to see unearthly, shouldering
up from three-story houses—

there comes the arch and weightiness of God;

so from God this endless
                        actionless itch to know
ourselves more real?—where we go, half-bent, under
the wind from inside the atom . . .
                        and still
they hang a boar by the heels, for the year's turning,
in the butcher's doorway.

                          And, over us, the saved,
come from the year's charmed round
of stars and labors, stand
still, with a child's small smile and even locks
for the wind to lift like hay;
and climb like children through the complicated
frail balconies, needing
a boost to the buttocks from the angel standing
below—
            while, opposite, the damned
discover everywhere mouths: a devil howling
to find his hand has clubbed into a crab . . .

But what does God see? This rictus facing nothing
in the scene that ends all things . . .
                            Only
the canceling-out of justice? Dante would say
He looks into Himself and there sees everything,
as everything, when it looks in love, sees Him—

a dance on a pinhead!

                    —though west and south,
in summer, toward the Cathar kingdoms,
everything divides, everything swallows everything
and lives inside it: the dancer's two
swivelling bodies meet in one head; the lion's
tail is also, seen closely, the crying woman's
arm . . .
                    and for an hour
one believes Dante, in the too tall grass.

Recitation for the Dismantling of a Hydrogen Bomb

From under the flat surface of the planet,
where we know, by statistics, you are waiting,
the White Trains sliding you through our emptiest spaces,
the small grassy doors to you trimly
sunk in the earth by desert or cornfield; then
the neat metal sheath, smaller than a mineshaft, with no
feeling of depth—
                    O how will you ever clearly
come to our sight? Surely our mortal hands
must take you, carry you, do, step by step, the terrible
laying you to sleep, or else—   There is no third way.

We have seen you, as in the mirror of a shield,
suddenly standing tall on so many sides of us
like beautiful ghosts—able to hold completely
still on your columns of smoke, then making
a slight lateral tilt to take direction.
And then we realized—everything standing, the rattled
watch on the table a-tick—we were the ghosts,
and you, your power, our inheritors.

And turning from the shield, we saw the world
glare back, withholding; as if a nothingness
already lived in bird and twig, and they
turned their backs on us, to know it.

                              But our minds
weren't ready yet; they could only wish and wish you
out of this world, out of ourselves.

    We might have thought of sending you
to wander, like a belled goat, the outer space
our fantasies wander so much now, caged
before the dreaming blips of our screens, inventing—
so we are told—a freedom untouched by you.
We would feel the endlessness you were shot into,
in which, if you destroyed,
past the range of our lenses, objects past our knowing,
it would come almost as a lightness, like the sense
of falling that comes before the fall of sleep.
It frees us without cheating you.

                         For we
are grieved to give up a power—as if time
began to run backwards, our bodies shrank and dwindled
until they reached our mothers' wombs, and disappeared.
Some days we'd even rather
use you, and use you up, than live the centuries
you won't quite vanish—the knowledge leaching through us
like your cores buried, after long debate,
in moon-polished canyonlands, always
a mile or so too near a major river . . .

The stars won't hide you. But there are precedents—
if analogy serves still—places
where things too big for us have been sung to sleep
once we knew we couldn't, or no longer wished to,
kill them.

        The flesh of death lay on the altar;
—or a class where doctors (the one who speaks a woman,
soft-voiced) teach those in permanent pain to focus
on one word, and cross their legs in the right way,
as if singing, silently, to the thing in themselves . . .

My Lord, good night.

So we set ourselves with sorrow down, to sing to you,
sing you from underground. First, of course, come
the treaties, the surveillance satellite cameras
pinpricking the globe—surface anesthesia
for our tireless fear of each other.

                Then
it is like taking up hands
against some larger shape of ourselves—the skull-like shield,
the outer fissionable cortex, the inner
strange sky of the lighter-than-air . . . The self-destruct
systems (and the circuits that spoke to them, under the mountains);
the temperatures, equalled only
"in transient phenomena like exploding
supernovae."

    My Lord, good night

                    —our arm
clad with the sun.

Go to sleep in us, as once, they say,
God went to sleep, and we trembled, not only that nothing
any longer overarched us, but that we
must contain what had.

                         (The class is quiet. The doctors
come and go unnoticed, on their beeping
emergency calls. We have gone so far into
what hurts us, whether incalculable nervous twitch
or cancer. Time drifts outside us. Then the voice
—Look at something. Anything. Our eyes open wider
than seemed possible, through blear hospital panes, on things
a little different for each. Brown canyons
of bark. Light combed out past them. End of winter.)

from **LOVE AND THE SOUL (1995)**

Epilogue

We will not see the gardens
of old age.
They were made for us,

but we got there too soon,
carrying our coffee cups into them
after breakfast, or at rest amid the daylong books,

with the fixed smiles
of those
who have outworn love's aggressions,

to see the other gardens
where love
is beyond aggression.

We were so strangely
afraid to enter them together,
as if, for all our tenderness,

we had married each other
in revenge, to destroy some hope in each other,
as only siblings

or parents should know enough to destroy.
Was that what we hid from, under
small names—

sharp, biting, moping but
consolable creatures? (Though yours
were always smaller, always slipping away . . .)

Lately I dreamed
we were lying, very ill, on our backs in an old house,
both of us

trying to die at the same moment.
There was no
terror, only an enormous exulting

sadness; then the instants, the itching
uncertainty, how one managed that, *to die* . . .
I thought of the other

dream, after the ultrasound, when our daughter
became real to us
(for weeks she bore her report name, "Normal Female"),

how we had bought a huge house
on the island
we walked parallel to for a mile, along the bayside

beach, picking up husks of horseshoe crabs,
that one happy weekend, shadowed
by your bleeding, the fear of miscarriage

(the happiness realized most under the shadow).
And in the house, a young man,
his arms raised and bunched, seemed to strive with the air

on the upper floor; while on the lower
old people, in a whiteness
of photos or cataracts, rocked and looked out to sea.

Would the dead
have been in it so much, if we
had known better how to fan the life in each other?

We had always defined ourselves
as the only people
capable of understanding each other's near-incapacity

for life, so well it alchemized
into that warmed, awkwardly brisk capacity
we displayed to the world.

That I—that we—had produced life
was like
the white unbreathable air of the upper ridges;

I quivered, the whole lung burned with it, I fell . . .
Not sayable. Underground
blankness. When I emerged from it

you had discovered, you
thought, that you no longer loved me.
I climbed out of it

daily facing your vision of the worst in me
as Dante pulls himself
out of Hell by the matted tufts on Satan's thighs,

only thinking he's descending
further, until at
last he stands free beneath the sky.

We seemed to have some agreement
that I would eventually
do the worst possible thing to you—

your dream-future
aloneness, flung in my face
yet yearned for . . .

For me, your anger,
read back, proffered a reason
why I could not—or would not—feel wholly released with you.

So in all things that descend
there is an in-
extricability, a pair of toothed gears, surface

causing surface causing . . .
—That New Year's, when the woman I left you for
dismissed me by letter,

Joanne said in the bar, "I don't think men and women
are meant to have relationships any more."
I thought of the computers

I was told about in Chicago,
that can be used but not explained, because their inner connections
will soon go faster than the speed of light.

—So the reactions fall from us,
understood, often, before we can even perceive them,
let alone call them back;

yet seeming so willful, sometimes, it takes years
to see they may have been
the only ones we could possibly have had . . .

There was so much that was ordinary and good between us.
I found that out the summer
I wanted to extirpate it, make it nothing,

and then looked up and
saw you: how your smile altered your face; your dogged
little-girl application, over the hooks and barbs

of Hebrew—a new language every summer . . .
And over you the books
you'd left for me to range, in so many houses . . .

That same August, my not-quite-lover
wrote me, "Thinking of leaving him, I still
ask his permission to go to bed at ten . . ."

—Like trying to chop a tree down, root by root,
that hopeless, until the last
frighteningly, emptily easy pull . . .

Even our first talk of this parting wandered
into memories of Europe
—our great risk, the treasure of our loneliness,

together and separate—coming at close of day
on walls the Cistercians
made an echo of the fog outside—dull, scouring whiteness . . .

Divorce was forgotten; passion
didn't exist. It was like wandering into
the dream before death, where everything is scoured

with a love like God's, because nothing one does any longer
affects it; the pain, now it's undemanding, radiant.
Writing poetry, one is free

—free for a moment—because one can hurl oneself
on that dream and still be alive.
(In that sense only, one writes instead of killing oneself.)

*But, I say, you can't live there. We move forward with
whatever moves forward with us. If that goes dead,
moving forward with it, we go dead ourselves.*

Then love becomes, incalculably, revenge . . .
But is that true? Is it reason enough? Our daughter
lives, this year, in books about the frontier,

Laura and Mary, blinding scarlet fever,
Indians appearing out of the flat horizon,
poison gas in the depths of the indispensable well . . .

You can see why: the danger simplifies.
Pa and Ma
won't look too long in each other's faces, calibrating

the terrible machinery; or into the neighbors' faces,
when they come by sled, perhaps once a winter,
and the Civil War ball gown is taken from its press.

Or were they wretched, and simply
afraid of the communal fear of using freedom?
Something is less simple than it ought to be . . .

Perhaps we both lacked courage,
preferring foregone disaster
to the terror of one single, limited thing.

Even—especially—in these last years
we'd rest on each other, sometimes,
when we suddenly came to peace from the long quarrels,

like swimmers
unable to move after hours in the dark lake;
or like *les Rois mages* of Autun, their crowns

so obviously too big for their one cape,
and the angel who wakes them with an almost shushing
gesture, as though true waking were still a sleep.

It seems so natural, now it will not happen
ever again. We leave it
as unbelieving

tourists leave a cathedral, half-relieved,
then sensing the heaviness isn't outside them but somehow
sinking endlessly through their veins . . .

There was a custom kept me
permanently too young, permanently old.
Life overarched and innocent—

how not feel losing it was half of death,
and the other half will never feel as
alien again?

Love and the Soul

Did you love her? I thought about her
continuously for a year. There were whole hours
there was nothing too thin about her look, her voice.

Did she love you? But it never counted against
any doubt or impulse of renunciation.

*

Only in the dark
could we listen clearly
to the voice that can say nothing but *I am good* . . .
I remembered Psyche, and how

I never wished to question
the god's masterful refusal to be known.
I had seen
too well, in their exact

afternoon light, the bright porticoes
which are the beloved, immaterialized;
and knew that, at midnight,
in the central chamber

what lifts the lamp, what tells her
anything she loves must be a monster
is not just "the human compulsion
to see, to know, the rejection

of whatever comfort derives from deception,"
but the soul's hatred and terror
of having all that depend
on the arbitrary contours of one flesh, one breath . . .

Another figure might be Stendhal's
of the branch
gathering crystals out of the cold water
at the bottom of a mine—

a girl drowned
in the shapeless, early depth within her man
the moment she takes on her specialness . . .
T. S. Eliot called requited love "the greater torment."

A man wanted to call the novel he never wrote that,
a man whose wife
kept dead mice and owls in the refrigerator,
to show just what they nourished each other by.

*

In what must be the misty, Northern
wandering of the story,
it is such small things—
a gold carding-comb, a gold thimble—

you are given with each failure,
each time you are told the place you want to go is
East of the Sun and West of the Moon . . .
But when the North Wind has spent itself and lies dying

having carried you to the castle
actually outside the universe,
it is these things that, given away,
let the soul enter; wake the beloved from false sleep . . .

Reading it out loud,
this morning of rejection,
I do not understand the story further.
I want it to be true;

not to have to believe
that what lights up the world from within is always the wrong thing;
that only struggle and limit
are the right.

Requited Love

1. Two People in Two Houses on a Hill

> *Il suo mister come mai, come mai fini?*
> —Puccini, *La Rondine*

Two people in two houses on a hill,
the same record playing, think about a mystery.
The record asks how it will ever end.
They feel its end could go round the earth and the seas
and are puzzled it doesn't get them past the steps to
the bay window with its view, the untouched telephone . . .
The summer hangs fire. Those they live with enter the room,
and they have to know them, get this visibly
under something, back on a shelf. Then they think of driving,
the car going out of control at some numberless pylon,
not because they don't want life, and partly just for the smash of it,
but mostly the suspension, like the moment on *Folle amore*
when the notes should dip, but instead
the voice seems to fade, and another space enters the music,
as if their stasis meant another dimension floating
black hole or angelic transparence alongside
the unreal life. *Come mai, come mai fini?*

2. April and May

A space I leaned away into. A space with a name,
or at least an initial. (You made me destroy your letters.)
You flirted with everyone. But you and I felt
the same thing about each other, from the same instant.

We had small, silent agreements. Your place on my couch,
the garden end, near the white shades. That we always drank Scotch.
The "I miss you" on the phone—the most you would say—and answered,
when necessary, "likewise" or "me too."

I was never sure I loved your face. It was so unseizable,
the eyebrows not the same distance from the nose, in the photo,
brown eyes only bright at the rims. And then it was all of it
wholly home, like the flat friendly Southern voice.

A voice like clear alcohol: things came out thrilling,
with a silvery ring of unstated laughter,
though you never raised it. One outwaited its silences
without a clue, as one waited the blankness of your eyes.

*

Then there were things I will never write about.
I want them to be a part of life forever,
and like life—like our love—to vanish whole,
mouths stopped and stopped with the dust of incompletion.

Yet would spare the wheeze you gave, when I made you happy
in our balked embrace: half-torn from your lips, and yet deeply happy,
as if you belonged to the sky, and it had spoken
something of how it felt to light this particular

earth: the delta of freeways; hillside; dust . . .

*

And I grew a face I could love. The most paralyzed days
the tenderness of its eyes startled me, in the mirror
and my body moved easily in its small postures of grieving
through the distancing house. I felt this could none of it harm me.

But to whom could I give it? You would have said, to God,
whatever you meant by that—absolute, neutral love
for all that is incapable of consolation . . .
"Even if you lose me," you had said, "you'll have me."

But I needed to hear your voice. There was nothing I meant by God,
unless it was the questionless power that let
you empty my life—a space, yet arrived so completely
the moment we said I must give you up forever.

3. Wires at Inspiration Point

With less conscience, or more courage, would the earth
refuse them so, pushing them upward? High over Berkeley

she likes the metal giants striding the hills,
so delicate, yet strong; and when you stand beneath them

there's a kind of click, or blip, when a phone call passes . . .
—Are they telephone wires, he asks. I always thought they

carried the main power between towns.
—Oh, she says. But did you know

if there's a bird on the wire when you make a call, it isn't
electrocuted until someone answers.

*

*—I had the fantasy you were inside me,
not just*—you know—*but all of you . . .*

*—The day I wanted you so much, I had the fantasy
I was you—my face your face, my hair your hair—*

*and all the while I went on desiring you. It's the same,
isn't it?*

—Stop that. You're breaking the rules.

*

Coming back the same way, they both hear it, under the bird-jabber,
a short, keen rasp, like cicadas; and even cupping

his hand to his ear, he still thinks it comes from the grass . . .
But a quarter-mile on, when she says, *if the world ends*

we'll have had this, for people
like us, the end of the world it always near

the black wires fly straight above them
and he hears it this time: clearly, from the air.

4. Letter to Santa Fe

    Staying over the three teaching days, to feel
our distance less: the aromatic dryness
when the heat recedes, the evening sprinklers going
on the desert-like, miniature-Midwestern lawns . . .
You like absences: will the high, wide air make you happy,
even after last week? Will N. be of help?
Will R. and E. take you to Bandelier,
where I climbed with my daughter to that smoke-hole, hardly
more than that, though a family lived or prayed there
(A. off somewhere, controlling her panic)—and felt the rock
stream back and back in itself, not knowing it meant how much in me
I didn't feel could come forward, not in this life.
    About Cather: she has two themes, the empty land,
and love, always irregular, always balked.
Like a treble and bass line at the farthest distance
that can still be heard as dialogue. The emptiness
always opens; then some tiny space is reclaimed.
The doctor lights his quartz stove, to read and not go home.
A boy and girl trade toys on the planks of the general store.
(They will still be doing that on p. 250,
when her husband blasts them back to—emptiness.)
    It's not fair to anyone, asking you to redeem
my steps there, two years back. It's too complex
why she was unhappy, and I was no help.
The red-earth dryness only told her how easily
one could die of thirst, that for me released an inner
fragrance in things. I think you and I could walk there,
our scrawny bodies somehow sure of carrying
enough in them to get us to the thin
stone lions almost shapeless with generations
of secret touching—overland pilgrims, by night.

And back? Or would we spoil it with our need
to be sure we had entered paradise? Too hard
to think of that now, or anything, when everything
seems to hinge on thought—
                              Love,

5. November and December

Last winter, before any of this started,
I used to think of you, waking up at three
and going to the bay window to console
yourself with its kingdom—three cities and the last ocean . . .
I thought if I were with you I could fathom
what made you unhappy, and feel what you felt, numbering
each light with its ring of pavement—beads of loneliness—
and you'd fall asleep, on the instant, on my breast.

If, at that hour, the phone rang once, then stopped,
I'd lie awake after, certain
you'd let yourself just dial, somehow knowing . . .

*

This fall, you want to watch me asleep;
it seems, you say, so unlike me. You are disappointed;
sleep eludes me by your side, the way our X-ray
speech escapes from normal conversation,
leaving us still
half-strangers when we talk of the day, the bread.

And your body, that's somehow held
such freedom for me, such rest—
isn't its childlike spareness
a strange blue jewel, closing on itself
in your quick, shallow sleep?

And then the night, with its violent, disembodying voices . . .

After the disco closes,
the black man's voice, searching the street's thinness
like the ring of a fallen trashcan lid: *You've got
to choose between us* . . .
And the voice that finally answers him, so quiet
sexless and far away—
a casual passerby? The hour I doze
it's your voice, shouting back at an accuser.

*If my love is not full love,
what use to me are the stars, those helpless fountains?*
Even as a child
I was afraid of the thought of them, like a clockhand, angling
all night past the black roofs . . .

I've wanted the moments
to stitch us together, in blood and nearness,
till I hardly knew your name—in a pause like sleep,
where our gradualness could at last be told from failure . . .

And in the morning, when the machine of me gives up trying
and looks out, your eyes, that seem to hold the weariness
for both of us
are open, watching: "You were possuming."

6. The Puccini Record Again, after a Year

In the life even now unbreakable, under glass,

we three sit and hear the bad soprano
falter through the *O to me descended
down from the throne of most high*

paradise—a wave in the sky, twice climbing
its fourths and sevenths, twice falling too low, then circling
back to the unresolving not-quite-center . . .

It's sung to her child, before going
behind the screen; but including
how love and Fate descended

in the same unsearchable, centerless wave . . .
You had trouble getting used to it, how the smallest
things were sung, not spoken; you still the outsider—scattered

imbalances of an opera evening with
a couple, new friends . . . (Your coughdrops. The plastic
champagne glass whose bottom somehow unscrewed and spilled.)

Two months later the violet in your eyes' dull brown
gathered for me; and what in another person
would have been a clear look, shook there

violently for the almostness. And for a year—
a wave in the sky—the past that did not happen
was allowed to happen: the high school breathlessness;

the *I can't imagine we have different thoughts*; your standing
outside my house at night, not caring about past or future,
hardly wanting to come closer than the wind . . .

How, from that, to "this sense of failing you
every minute I'm with you . . ."
Music, we know, is always bigger

than a person. That's why there are those Cupids
on proscenium arches, reclining
in a space no foot could climb to, and no hand

touch, across air . . . Could you have flung yourself
like a long high C, and not had some lack of gravity
that would suddenly turn away, find it not worth trying.

and writing, in your classroom cursive, "miss
the good times," for fear of giving anything
legibly cancel the "miss," and put "remember."

A note too high was struck, and a house vanished;
a note too high was struck, and a life vanished,
even to the white cloth shades

I liked to place you under, the mild
clear nights of that paralyzed winter, so your hair
would play on the luxury of their odd brocade.

In our last weeks together, I actually wished for
the next life you believed in,
where I saw your eyes were clear, and able to hold . . .

There's no good reason, no
resolution. Close-ups of singers
are always disturbing: the whole face

skewed by the exaggerating, naked pleasure
of the enormous mouth—
unlike actors, who can present

the desirable, because they always watch who's watching back . . .
—Safe in our house that night, after you drove home,
she said, *You always know*

someone will die bloodily, that's what
gives it its keenness. And though I might have said, no,
it's the unspeakable value, the icon of love,

that makes her death
itself the tragedy—nothing more said or sung—
it's sheer luck no one died from all of this.

No one took from it more
than one carries through death: although
I seem to have been given, permanently, the tears

that surprised me so
when I came back to you, out of doubt and distance;
that moved you so much

you leaned down and licked one off my face.

Fragments: Traveling in Marriage

I. THE ETRUSCAN COUPLE IN THE VILLA GIULIA

They have not shown themselves as lovers; neither
as dark-winged Fates to each other.

That's how the young couple knew they were theirs, the moment
they approached them, down separate, angling corridors:
turned a little aside from each other, the man too thin
for his great height, and a faint irony curling
his lip forever; the woman ample, settled
in the glow of baked earth, in the four talkative braids.

They have not died from knowing each other; they show it
by lifting the cup encouragingly
to the invisible friends who never leave them,
whom they've persuaded
to stay so late, that even these two have slipped
out of the glass and taxicabs of Rome
to hear their last story, and catch the fine
familiar reflex with which
she takes the last sentence from his lips, to end it—

who perhaps, in the dark to come, will love each other
at last wholly, forgiving: a red-earth glow.

2. LANDFALL

Peace of weary-edged tenderness. They choose a house.
How hard for each of them to live. Respect goes on forever.
The inset benches, the brick patio, the strange stalks
brown-bare, then all white flowers, then bare again. Like England
or old age, so carefully made. You couldn't leave it
if you wanted to, because you couldn't finish counting
what there is to leave: snowdrops suddenly
outside the January study window, gnats climbing their narrow
invisible ladder, when there's enough dusk in the air . . .
And so they do what they can: argue the pictures
to the almost right place on the wall, and scrape the moss
from the brick's almost facial weathering, so the deck chairs
can go out on it, so that one day a quiet-mannered
visitor will come and her child spill her odd, unflowery
perfume playing with her purse in the Craft-style bathroom.

Domestic Architecture

There is no reason to be unhappy. Purplish flowers
star the twigs out your window; it has a stately frame,
eight small panes in procession above the great one,
brown mullions like musical bars. And if the neighborhood's
not what you asked for, still . . . Such things have woken you
at almost every age; what is there more?
But your life was unarraigned then, protected by others,
and the day moved inside that, in its small panes.
And if what protected also imprisoned, made a sameness?
Now the first hope is gone, you'd say you did it
for honesty: to say what you meant about longing,
not half-adapt to one you were still half-failing,
and so be taller; so, perhaps, break open
what was knotted inside . . . Now, your lover brings strangeness
like many jewels on the dressertop overnight.
You are trying to build each other a shelter in the larger
spaces of your hearts. You don't feel safe for an hour.
There are so many gaps that can open. When she sees
the cracks in the ceiling and not the stately window;
when you see the ranch-house blankness and not the elm
she turns to, waking, the wind has a chance to start blowing
that says birth to death is a single plain; there was never
a house on it, not a tree, not a pluckable purple flower.

Wide-Angle Shot: Return to Snowy River

When she leaves her father for him, the landscape changes—
the incredible drop-offs at their feet, the pointed
after pointed ranges, near-bald with stones—

aren't just a way of not showing sex, its monumental
suspensions the body sometimes expresses, sometimes not,
oddly aslant the heart;

but pure portrait of contact, pure portrait of danger,
and the old claim, that all of life is in that,
the infinite stopped at its feet . . .

It's clearly all we have yet: contact, risk;
though love, as always, finds odd nails to hang
itself on—yogurt for breakfast, the ironing board . . .

Little stammerer, your monumental
silences before the downdraft of these things,
and what boils up from them always, the unlovely

intractable *I*—cliffside
paths I wander with you as if they were the years
from your age to mine, loving what endangers me . . .

Then your words hooked, torn—lone eagles—over depth—

Deb's Dream about Pavese

I.

He had a long red scarf shielding his throat
(looking the way he does in the last photo)
and it scared you, because it was fire-colored, and like a snake.
But he said (in Italian, but you understood),
Take it, it will take the fever away;
so you gathered as he unwound, and woke up better.

To me he says, *One nail drives out another
but four nails make a cross.
I will be a diabolical friend to her.
We are given only what we ask for with indifference.
The thing most feared in secret always happens.*

He says in the wastefulness
of going from person to person, the feelings
never in balance, the universe
slides off toward extinction—a man
no more than the rumpled smells of his
unacceptableness. Only a fool
clings then to the look he had to
misinterpret. And the woman
is as helpless as the man. (His anger is that
of total Need. Does he know
if it were less absolute, his prick would stand?)

I cannot refute him. But something healed you.

2.

If it were that old story
of searching for the other half of you through the world,
the odds wouldn't be good, but there'd be a logic—
but it's more like
the body of Osiris, one right thing glimmering
in each person, as if swallowed by mice or fish . . .

—It could go another way. To bed too quickly,
with lots of giggling. Later she's sensible, "slow," her coolness
hurts him; or she's sure
he'd be bored in the end. And still, it's a little marriage,
describing the moonlight, waking up early to wind,
coming home at night to camomile tea.

—*In New York now a lot of people are almost*
asexual. Disease and, I don't know, the meeting people . . .

Because all loves are not the one love they are meaningless.
Because all loves are the one love they are real.

I see the scarf, where it curves through all of them,
like DNA, like Isis finding
here the clear look, there the touch that grazes
and gives your skin back its childhood softness, though it goes—
the story longer told to each new person, but each time
told by someone different, each
time a window . . . (*But when*
does one get to what one holds to, what one doesn't lose?)
I must pick it up, where he threw it in the dirt,
the pointless cellular chain.

Your Forest-Moonlight Picture

Unbroken sea surface, swelling and changing,
as if a small plane were scanning it—breathing mists,
breathing pure paint, slash and shimmer, and no horizon;
or star-material, roiling, metal, gray . . .
Then the mute funny thing you'd drift above it,
ball-bearings, rope, a bicycle, an O—
never explaining, nothing linking down.
For a few days it was our forest, the sea was moonlight—
hunter's moon—before as well as behind it,
and real black branches you could be lost or found in . . .
Then I was gone; the surface was repainted
hard sea, the branch, like Dante's, grew small thorns . . .
You watched me all the way down the road from your door,
as if I couldn't help getting smaller and smaller.

Toward the New Year

(Lower Manhattan)

1.

The sharper numbers slipping upward. Rains
leach a whole past of snow
from the black streets. Weightless acceptance,
though the bridges still tear the long perspectives upward
like iron muzzles, of some afterworld . . .
—How could a whole city be washed of such
love, of such terror?
(And the man in the subway, flattering, peddling his roses—
but no one has said *your wife*
of any of the others . . .)

2.

But they won't stop rising . . . Lying down at last, between
"necessary" and "not permanent"—and how much farther
the night might drift us, even when exhaustion
shelved us like twin rock strata underground . . .

Was it the way the sirens sifted upward
(the firehouse roofs below), floors, rungs past our high bed,
made me see them as rising through, above us—
numbers like dawn birds, more and more, till they stop, taller,
whiter than cities, with our separate names.

The Ambivalent Man

He works so hard to make each moment perfect,
but underneath there's always

a kind of negative forming, to be developed
in the salt of his solitude; an accuser saying

everything she said was boring or mean-spirited,
he was never comfortable with her for an instant.

Of course, she may simply be the wrong person.
There are always reasons
anyone he would choose is the wrong person.

*

Was that why—their first walk
out on the pier, the day choppy, facing the ocean—

she spoke of the courage
of those who once set out on it, in their creaking boats?

*

When all he can want to say is *stop it stop it*,

he thinks of what he would like
to be happening instead,

and sees himself lay his head
on her bare shoulder,
and have her understand something
from so far back, he can only catch the blue
edging toward lavender—
and not words, just a series of enlarging silences . . .

And then he thinks perhaps this *was* the memory:
the eye-path crossed and went elsewhere, the receiving face
could no longer be known, or loved.

*

But what, when the nerves, that make the words misfire
between them
are the very thing that, watching her cross a room—

that tissue of hesitations, flinch at being visible,
plus a certain doggedness, as if
her face were having to push a heavy boulder—
he sees with his whole body, he's way inside
like being inside a tree.

*

She says, *the anglerfish,*
because the male not only spawns but lives
inside the great, glistening, open globe
of the female's vagina . . .

When he feels right about her,
people mountains trees
all slip back into their right, beautiful place.

*

He thinks if he could make her a gift
even of the pain she is in him. That's why he chooses

the statue of the convulsed man, half-emerging
from the body of a frog; that's

why he leaves
the copy of Kafka face down on the table.

*

She has learned not to trust the tears
that well in his eyes, as if
seeing had become a warmer, closer thing . . .

They say he is too happy to have persuaded himself;
they say he will say anything
just to go on being there, in the moment, one.

*

She will tire of it, in the end.
That way, he will still be the victim.
He will never be the one who has rejected someone.

*

She will go by his apartment to pick up something.
He is playing Madame Butterfly; it sounds as if
it has been playing for days.
But what he says is, I do better alone.

      *

And what if the negative tells the truth?
—Tells him he's come to something
known long ago, meager
and dark to itself beneath the
apparent sweetness?
What if his kindness was only
an old complicity
with his own undoing,
his estrangement the saving lamp?

      *

Or, he steps out onto it.
That metaphor. Bridges. Ships.
The ground giving one way or another
at every move.
The constant ringing—does everyone hear it,
making things strange as a dream?
He doesn't know if he's bored. He is very scared.
He takes another step.

Forest Street

So what if, days after, he couldn't look into faces,
and the morning light was itself a face, an eyelike moistness
beading, if it came early, the knobs of his poor chairs,
driving him back into dark, his sheets like downward wings . . .

And if someone told him C. S. Lewis's heaven
was like that, *so sharply real*
it would hurt the feet of the damned,
he would know he could marry, needing that balance,
that insistence on reality, so his body
could stand with another body, in the light.

For what else was there?—the bars' delusion,
all eyes and no eyes, the slipping-space between creatures,
the night-cool breathing
its waver into the air, at ten in the morning . . .

But there was something else: a cry, true distance?

It's not that the loneliness was part of it—
the almost accidental girl, the round
red rug of the summer rental—
still there, I walked past it this year, in the stick-storm of Cambridge Victorian—

but without the loneliness he wouldn't have felt it,
not, at any rate, at that age—

in her slipperiness the endless interval,
the *tender indifference,* as if a traveler
should pass, once only,
through a street all shined gray stone in the early morning . . .

And when it's all gone, every face disassembled
from these addresses, what's there might be what he felt
after, in the real street, passing the islanded streetlamps—
under light bright as paint, translucent pulp of leaves;
under the real paint of the garages, wood
and the watery flicker of rot, wood that would again be earth—
something his body discovered
it was part of, something that went down
within itself forever
and vanished there.

Rilke's Argument with Don Giovanni

I never thought
I'd be anything like you . . .
I was drawn up, as in a whirlwind, by their gaze
and wished to live there forever—a soul around my soul—
astonished, perhaps, to be wanted there at all—

who was Mitzi in the army; the boy fainting by the wall at school.

But then, when the wincing *not right*
began in my head; when I wanted
so much to be loved in the moment I found my separateness
still there, still real—I needed
the one who could be told anything, even the thing
that drove her away.

People will say I disliked the body; it's the easiest
explanation, for someone who talked with angels.
But my dear ones will know something different,
how astonished and careful
I could be, like a boy
given something unbelievable,
the pale gold flare at the bottom of the stream.

The men of our time burst into them
like the brusk hussar
at the dressing-room door in Strauss's *Ariadne*.

I loved their talents
as if they were my own talent,
a surer hand to reach the brush, the page—
transfixed with knowing
how a child shapes itself, will-less, in the dark.

And they must have felt something heavy in me, too rich,
too complete in itself. They dreamed
stronger dreams in my presence.
But the weight was what sank, what even I couldn't hold.

I always hoped the right one
would arrive like wind,
that freshly, instantly touching everywhere.
I never remembered
the nature of wind is to pass by.

I'm glad to think of their oval portraits in my biography,
soul on soul on soul,
clouds and clouds of them, lace and hairpins—
and I whose soul could vanish
at a spastic's tic on a curb's edge in Paris.

I pray they weren't what yours were—
things
flung in the face of the echoing man of stone.

The Author Reconsiders

Of course I look back on the first parts with amazement.
Adultery is a coffee-table book. As for being *angry*
that your first, dream-darkened choice
didn't mesh just right; and found someone else who did . . .
Then that other stuff: *A Sad Heart at the Singles Bar?*
But perhaps a feeling is measured by the newness
brought to it: the walk past the crest, by the freeways—
that hunger of bare hills
eating the world to origin and finality—
were what they seemed, if only because I had never
lived so purely, outside the rules. But the old life stayed—
it too possibility, it too unlived.
If one friend speaks of "certain old arrangements
that don't hold good any more,"
another friend says, "They say you did the worst thing,
you, the 'innocent' one, bringing her there
in the house with your wife, pretending to talk about poetry . . ."
What I mind most, in these pages,
is having said so little to explain
why things darken so quickly, between men and women,
and not just in marriage; how soon,
after the sheer balloon-like luck of the party,
they're so huge to each other, niggled-at, unappeasable . . .
The man, we're told, all fist, drawn in from the sensed cold
until every thought is counterargument;
the woman hammering and hammering, so unshakeable

her sense of powerlessness, at his ear, like a locked door in a dream;
her dread of being overshadowed; his conviction
that, whatever outsiders may think, the dark strike-back
she's drawn from him at last is, as she'll say, his true
nature unveiled, distilled; all that leads back to
nolo contendere, that odd plea in law courts
that gives up the chance to look innocent, pays the penalty
whatever it is, sure it's the smaller cost . . .

Unanticipated Mirrors

(In Memory of Alfred Satterthwaite)

1.

Leave the doors open, the poet says, *the whole house*
open all night, so we may die
a little here, in us, and there in him
we live a little. Before anyone died here
this house stood open. I could see from the darkness
Isabel and her sister shelling peas
at either end of the long walnut table.
She told me I should work for a newspaper that summer,
how she'd loved that—the glimpses into other lives . . .
The weak light hung cloudy, pregnant, in the dark wood,
as if a house could be the summer night
brought indoors, flickerings, blowings-back of white
curtains, unanticipated mirrors.
Then Alfred came downstairs, and brought my story.

2.

Why wasn't I angry? He said just what my father
might have said: you couldn't tell, I might fail as a writer,

I'd still make a good scholar . . . Out of the depth of leafage
an explanation presses, a signature like the wound
in the horse-chestnut flower. I was living that sense
that even—especially—unhappy love gives
of seeing things twice; seeing for the absent other.
And in that double sight, I saw the failure
was his, and was not evil; ploughed back under
into—what?—as the night-smell takes back everything—
the open doors, the glass in his hand, the eyebrows'
Mephistophelean dance over the eyes' pure, black
astonishment at life . . . And saw, too, that my seeing
might be plowed under; or, in me, live and grow.

3.

To pass into a house, as into a mirror;
to see what the grown-ups wouldn't show us, the wrestling
with their own pasts, with each other, the dignity down—
fighting us too, often enough, fleeing the ghosts
of unwritten books . . . but accepting our chaos too, our failure.
So it's always a little the house in detective stories,
in the candlelight after the great crime, when faces—
even one's own, especially the beloved's—
yaw and flicker into unsearchableness.
And it has its real ghost, a young one, I've feared and hoped
to meet again, these open-windowed nights; who lived here
when he failed his Comps and his father threw him out,
two years before he fell/jumped? under the train,
So *Grave. Wilderness.* (More poets.) But also *Paradise.*

4.

In the detective stories, too, we turn
to some opposite of the Father—
some cocaine mainliner, some grim divorcé
or fat man (even too-perfect Lord Peter
has his shellshock; the story requires an almost
unmanning)—to show, by the light of his funny pain,
where evil is: not where the Fathers said, in the moment
we forgot their existence, suddenly only ourselves;
but the slower loneliness when that isn't somehow
caught back, accepted, until one chilled heart
thinking it only calculates, revenges . . .
I felt my life balance among other lives—
the shape of an adulthood we could enter
without maiming ourselves.

5.

Dick's been cleaning this house for weeks—the fireplace ashes
you just threw, these last years, at the foot of the cellar stairs,
you'd given up so . . . and the suicide letter
in case Isabel died first—but addressed *to* Isabel . . .
And *So what*, at the last, we sit here saying.
You gave us, I said when you died, chaos and warmth,
the mystery of their balance. When Joel's father
tracked him here at last—I can hear it in your mouth—
"He was standing in the front doorway, and he said,
'I should have beaten him more, when he was a child'—
and he could have had me to court then, easily—
I said, 'Dr.—, you are a son of a bitch.'"

And so released us; for the young always know they're
murderers, if only of their pasts.

6.

And if we too served your needs—wounded relivings
of youth, escape from work, from the loving war with each other—
So what, we say again. *The house must be left open*,
the poets have said it, *the tower built without stones*.
The thin walls of this house are old. A farmer set these
orchard trees out in the huge planetree dark
that makes the nights so endless. I like to think
his stern God lost himself and then came back
in this quicksilver loosing of the boundaries—
the young not young, the old not old, but life
flaring in its quick resin on itself,
one clear thing like the round-filled glass of sherry,
chaos that keeps the circle unconfining—
the smoke-breath lasting, hosts and guests asleep.

Enthusiasm

Someone said, *your poems lack enthusiasm,*
and was afraid half the story
would die of that. So I went back
to Charlottesville, five paces north from the fireplace,
faint-fragrant in the hot weather, then west into
the cramped dining-room, as if that would bring me to us
practicing the modes of caring
our hands still knew as one, in spite of our minds—
in from bedding out marigolds in the clingy clay,
or sitting together, the long afternoon,
rounding and rounding the small, egg-shaped pieces,
orange carrot, pale turnip, for *navarin printanier.*
There would be white straight rain and sudden thunder,
it being Virginia, it being summer,
so that later, in the cool, the dining-room table transported,
largesse of candles and friends on the screen porch, into the dark . . .
And next day come so soon, *day falling through day through the screen door* . . .
And so autumn: the heavy pear orchard of the stars;
the birdseed bright as salt on the rare ice,
and seven purple finches; the robin on the first of March;
the ashtree that was our guardian and the moonlight
you wanted to stay out in, for your poem
where it walked through the houses and left them all one house,
transparent, unthreatened; and I, too often, nervous
of trying to hold the moment, dragged you in.

Highway Restaurant

We all have places we step out of time and are perfectly happy.
This is one of mine. Perhaps because it's a place
where I can be grown-up yet have my childhood,
or because it took me so long to feel good in public alone,
without self-consciousness, chattering in my head,
that even looking at the bad mural with the mileages
to the cities, even lifting my water glass, is fun.
We all choose people in such places, though we feel we like everyone;
I choose the young waitress
who thinks her nerves are part of the other life, and invisible,
and doesn't see what spare beauty they give each moment, here;
and the man—they're about thirty—so obviously pleased to be with the woman,
though she's fleshy and somehow sick—anyway, takes pills before dinner.
And I think I know, apart from whoever *I'm* missing,
why I choose them. They're riding rip-currents of the present;
they say we're in our flesh, our nerves, as in a river,
and it may take years to master—or it may drown us tomorrow.
And I've heard today that a man I've respected, but never known well,
has a form of cancer with 20 percent chance of survival.
And though it would be very foolish, defensive, and tempting fate
to say I don't care how many more years I live,
that's like what I feel. The highway is a river,
exhaustion in it is beautiful, and our gathering here—
so much larger somehow, almost family—
has something of a fast-forward of all the gathering
and losing in our lives.

You can't quite say it: the joy comes from somewhere,
and while that doesn't prove we'll ever
wake up in a different river, in the sky,
it just might prove there's an object equal to joy,
and if we don't hold it any one place, it's only because it needs
so much to be everywhere . . .
Like the waitress. How I'm too shy to say more to her
("More coffee?" "Please." A good sunset's over,
the long, flimsy curtains drawn . . .)
but when I go up with the check the girl at the cash register
sees her scrawl on the back and says, "Lisa Ann. She's *fun!*"

For My Daughter, Leaving

Dearest, I would not want you to forget
this place, though it was never home to me
till too much drama made that not the question . . .
Palms and winter camellias; the seasonlessness gathering
to the ocean-light focus of the winter solstice;
the Craft tiles with florets and knights in armor;
or even the street where I moved, its flat-glare bungalows . . .
The schools where you learned so much about Native Americans,
so little after 1790; the summer trips north with Grandma
to the long white twilights, the brother-killer-whale,
the ratty spruce drooping and stretching, the whole coast curving
round, like its own looped makings, to Japan.
To tragedy, serenity. Balance unlike our world,
its *happiness*, its *failure*. Which were we?
Puzzles gathered dust on the hall table. Before
we had a vacuum cleaner, before the crumbling
undercarpet was up from the one room I lived in,
we had fish. They swam so far beneath us—
your stoic face; my distracted anguish about women—
we could hardly guess their ills. Then one had dropsy,
its intestines came out through its anus and wouldn't go back.
I learned, that day, how you put down a fish.
You stun it in cold water, then wrap it up
in wet kleenex, so it won't suffocate,
then put it in the freezer.
That way it just dozes off, the pet stores say.

When you found out what I'd done, we had to rewrap him
in a Christmas cookie tin, with herbs and ribbons.
That was the beginning of the Goldfish Graveyard.
Even daubed on with white house-paint—"Princess
a special fish," "Silverstreak," "Little Arrow,"
"Good Fish"—this one a mass grave, short-lived prizes
from a school fair—their names didn't last the rainy season.
But a garden of worn bricks sprang up amid the thyme
and free-landing poppies; mint; ineradicable blackberry;
the tramped-down paths making a tiny center.
You could never quite tell how people would respond.
Most girlfriends liked it, but one of the kindest
called it Auschwitz for fish. You could see her point—
a culture, like so much in culture, built on
the premise of small things neglected till they died.
But she was the one who gave us Lumpy,
the only fish who rises to his name.
She hadn't fed him much, so he just kept growing
until someone else told me about a goldfish
that ended up a foot long, and I got careful.
(She hadn't named him, either. His twin, Bumpy, died.)
I pray he will never lie here, his tail will bend,
too big for the cramped corners, but a sign of
something—a flowing, a freedom—when I
have moved him to newer, airier rooms; when you
come back from the sharp autumns of your new city.

Tidepools

1.

How near the shore the blue
gathers again in the water after breaking,
cobalt and electricity in the clearness . . .

But withheld now, upending these
little homes, little bits of the inner salt of daylight,
separate a few hours so we can see

that first idea of flesh, the sponge's
live carpet on the inner face of rock,
touch and play-flinch from the devouring flowers . . .

How grave and attuned your small face gets,
so I also see, without blame or forgiveness,
what it was not in my clouded look to mend.

Yet you seem to like me best here, crossing
the high-tide island, its wave of uninhabited grasses,
saying, *Daddies are good at outdoor things.*

And we hold the names together, *chiton, nudibranch,*
as they rose, once, from the page
in the aromatic shore house, in the desklamp's pincer,

Blake's icicle of Creation, passionless
as the light is, also, for the man returning
from all the journeys; from the journey of knowing fate.

2.

When the second life came from within my body,
at fourteen, fifteen—how I hated this; how I wanted
the Midwest opening

its joyful elm towns
to our returning journey,
like crossed swords above the joyful bride and groom;

its humid light in which things grew so densely
it seemed space could curl inside itself forever
and a birdcall still shoot through, unimpeded—

like a life filled with friends and saying more
unguardedly right than you thought the day had room for,
and more always to step out of the stillness;

and as the small creatures know they move more safely
for the infoldings,
so at night the dancers, unimpeded,

hardly feeling the need to touch each other . . .
It seemed then one could be mixed with something unknown
but unbetrayable.

It seemed there was an act that was a preparing for death,
and the crickets knew it, with their intermitted
falterless ratchet, down by the grass-stems, near autumn . . .

The moment would come, after years, when they would catch me—
brimming, then stopping; without
measure, without doubt—and the explanation of the world

couldn't hold me more.
They seemed to say, *you have not done your preparing;*
but it is only one action, so there is always time.

3.

Suzuki Roshi
says if you could think with a frog's mind,
through and through,

you would be Buddha.
But what unremitting steadiness
of wind the cormorants know themselves by, plunging

to their guano island . . .
Do seals feel warm or cold?
And Steinbeck's "tidepool Johnnie,

growing weak and perhaps
sleepy as the searing digestive acids
melt him down . . ."

—A friend perhaps dying. Transparency
through which childhood
shows more, its sadness

never wholly readable . . .
(Was it because it was lonely,
or you knew, even then, it would end?)

And the midwinter light
that beats up so low, but sharp, off the ocean's mirror,
the headlands velvety,

translucent with new green: as if that light
took them up with both hands
to give back to the sun.

4.

I haven't mentioned my father's grave,
a few sand dunes away, where every second
or third visit you, who never knew him,

like to place the smoky-purple flowers . . .
If *a child's life
is punishment for the father's*—the slow turning

outward of the wounds that he kept hidden,
but more grotesque now, so that reason cannot help one
live around them, not

live them through; and not through healing when we die . . .
What will hold then (not, surely, the comforting
map of the years, the "successes")

against the glare
pouring in from farther than we can imagine,
salt plants enduring it, killdeer alighting?

But the vastness is in us, too, the rising and falling.
When I have managed to forget
everything but my breath, the story has touched me

at all points at once, its clangors
and bright screens.
      I used to envy the dead
in urban graveyards, in summer,

for how much life swam back
in on their dark: a car horn
in the street, the shiny fence-hafts, the humid elms . . .

If I love someone enough
I might end there, or anywhere, losing my self
in a place that is *ours*, an endlessly inland.

If not, I am willing to be salt and sand.

from RES PUBLICA (1998)

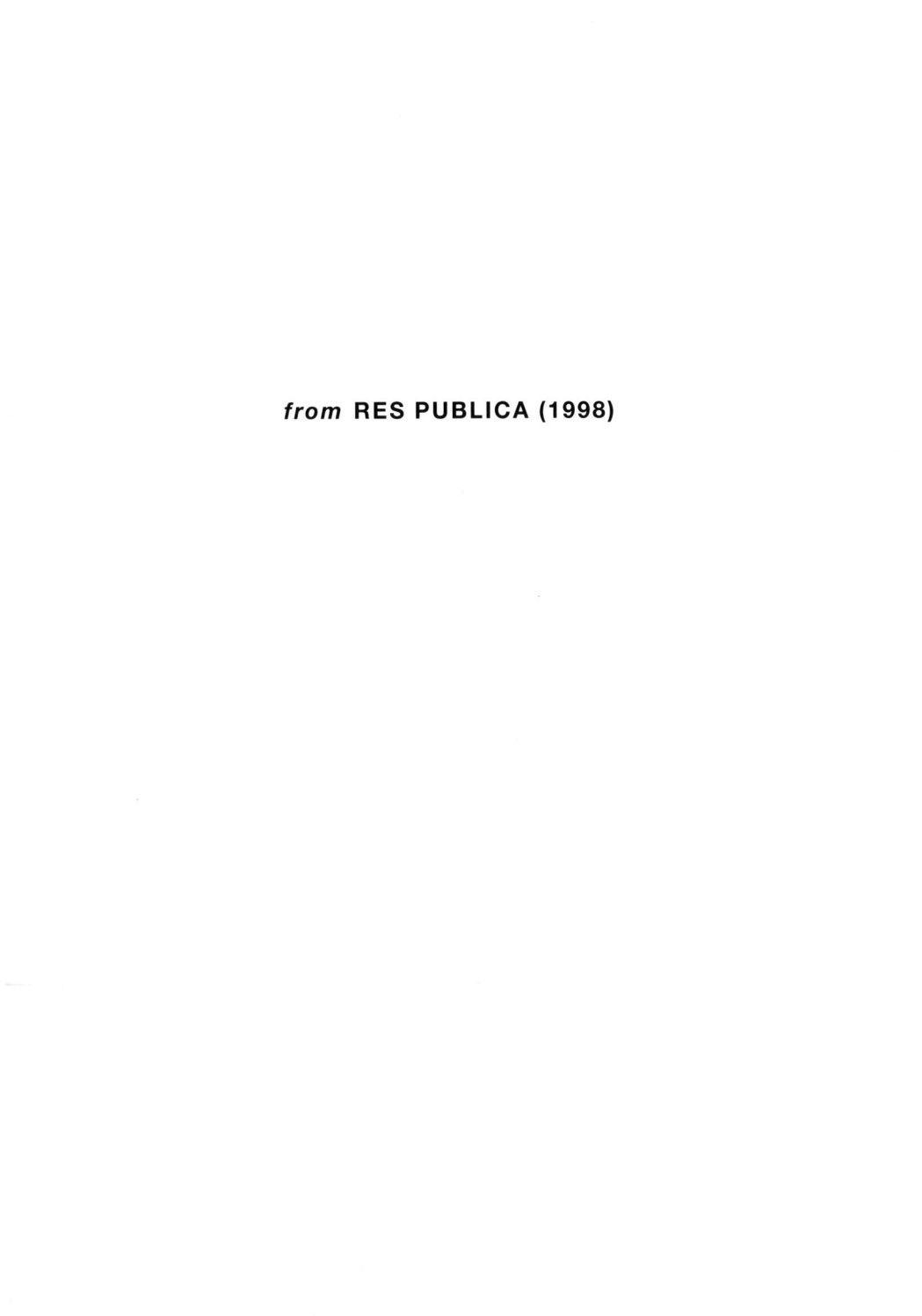

A Childhood Around 1950

Sometimes a horse pulled a wagon down the street.
A knife-grinder sometimes knocked at the back door.
Airplanes passed over. Put to bed in the poignant
half-thereness of summer twilights, we followed their long wobble
into Midway, rare and slow as dragonflies.

New kinds of safety. Our parents held their breath,
though sickness, for us, was the vile yellow powders
that burst from the capsules we had to gulp, and couldn't.
The new danger quiet in the milk and air.

The electric chair troubled no one. Good and evil
were stark things, as grainy movies made the dark.
But the city stopped if one of us was stolen,
and found thrown, days later, in a forest preserve.

It was what was. A childhood always is.
Fathers came home at noon and took off their hats.
Later, streetlights . . . But who was that *lamplighter*, in the stories?
And we went on living it, like a wave, that doesn't know
it is at every moment different water.

Dreams of Sacrifice

(Chicago, April 1968)

I saw them coming, waves of them—from the West Side
we'd watched burning on TV—up the dim treads
in the tarnished-gold light I'd loved, if I were honest,
every year of my life; then down the landing,
yelling, brandishing, surging, toward our door . . .
And saw myself come out, chest bare—
not really, but as if my heart walked bare before me,
saying, "Take me for all of us, wash me, make me yours,
make me pure enough to do your will for all;
or if not, kill me."

              Three weeks later, they (well, one of them)
did kill someone like me, and my parents heard it,
the lone shot the bicyclist fired, that sent the body
crumpling against the railing of my old school.
They were "sick" that they "mistook the shot for a backfire."
And, perhaps because I'd been so absolute,
that spring break, about fascist "Amerika,"
they sent me the clipping, the faces. Though he'd had little
enough sympathy for me, when he used to watch
white toughs dog me home along that same

spear-pointed fence, my father wrote, "the victim,
a benevolent student . . ."

                                      I suppose the face reminded me
too much of my own, pudgy, irresolute, *in search of*,
ashamed of, innocence—so I wrote, needing
to *make claims* for the hungry bones of that other face,
tilted up to police lights, floating, high,
whose *single beauty* lay in killing *one
for one, one for the shared, blurred guilt of all.*

My father, too, it seemed, needed some way
to place himself. Already ill,
he walked out the half block, one quick May night,
"to see the spot where trees cast a dense shadow."
I imagined *blackness lay focussed*, for him,
like a body crumpled there; and wrote my poem
to prove his dark was created by light,
light looking *too tenderly* at itself—the windows
of our building bent back that way, by the crenellations—
light streaming on his back, what he wouldn't see, the *clue* . . .

When you're young, your world's imposed on you, so powerful
against you, you think it's all-powerful, forever—
easy enough to side with its destroyers.
But when it's half-vanished, and freighted with
everything you've loved and achieved within it,
easy to make of love and achievement a fist, to smash
whatever hurts your world . . .

                                     Avalokiteshvara
split his head in ten, with meditating
on the ways of suffering. In the old bronze,

you can see the heads dangling, like bluebells on a stalk,
the eleventh flowering on top
because, the way they tell the story, the Buddha
could still put them back together, and add his own.

Paint It Black

It was clearer then
how there's a depth in longing
nothing ever reaches. Geoffrey and I sat up talking

in the bare apartment, the streets
sunk beyond leaf-depth
in their two, three hours of absolute

quiet. I was angry
because I'd botched something—the very
drunk, beautiful teenaged townie

bound for Goucher in the fall
who drove us harrowingly up over
brick sidewalks, whose focus

on me I didn't pick up on till too late.
Geoffrey thinks, in such cases,
you don't get a second chance. Perhaps

I'm more restless than really angry,
the way, in the oddly triumphant drive
of *Paint It Black*, that summer,

you never know what—
infidelity, death?—has made him
want to see, where her face was, the Black Sun.

(Later, I'd see her
laughing too much, in the coffeehouses,
with a skeletal African dancer

suspected, next year,
of rifling purses and lifting my twenty-first birthday watch
at another "open party.") But for now

it's very late. The dew
gathers on the strange backyard power-stations,
on every rotting plank of the three-deckers.

Suddenly a long shaking
comes through the ground, followed
(measurably) by a clap like thunder. Next day

we'll learn it was liquid hydrogen
in the Electron Accelerator at Harvard
two blocks away. Four technicians

critically burned—like sacrifices
in the underground caves
of Teotihuacan where the snake-faces

conch shells and wave-signs climb the stairs to the sun.
What I can't forget
is how, when it happened, when we ran

outside to nothing at all—dawn beginning—
I knew I'd been
waiting for it, some coded

burst from the core. These small hours
I think of the years (*X*'s breasts
that made me feel no straining, but like a tree

outfeathering; *Y* imaginarily
glimpsed in the museum) and still
reach down for it, hand under

the roots . . .

Listening to Leonard Cohen

(driving south from Charlottesville, January 1993)

In the dawn of time I lived on a little hill.
It was green even in January, green up to
the doorstep where, short weeks later, a miniature
hyacinth would come. The lines of the house were neat
as a jewelbox, from which, in the pearly, brooding days,
freshness had spilled. And, of course, we who lived there
found ways to be unhappy.
                         *All men would
be sailors* in those years. They wanted the landscape
to fold to a wave-length; wanted not to know
when they woke in the morning, which state's light was broken
through the slant pines. Wanted the afternoons
in shade-pulled rooms to bring girls whose eyes
were that wide with possibility, shocked free; whose very names
they wouldn't learn. (And the women wanting?—not that,
but not to be kept in houses.)
                         And we, who'd begun
to hold still, like our parents, half from fear,
half from hope of taking root—
after Altamont, after Manson, we were afraid
of our own side, no less than of their opposites

who looked just like them, mountain men, the dirty
runnels of time their beards.

*There is a grain of sand in Lambeth that Satan cannot find
Nor can his Watch Fiends find it tho' they search numbering every grain*
(But who were the Watch Fiends? And was it here, on the hill,
or only there where everything changes?) *for within
Opening into Beulah every angle a lovely heaven . . .*
Playing perhaps as I sat reading this, *heroes in
the seaweed, children in the morning*—
                            making me wish for a guide
to the spaces inside the moment, someone I loved
without having to love her, because she
was water wave-length madness *oranges from China,*
the river's endless answer out her door . . .

And so, to the open-air rock bands; at the medievalist's
old stage-inn lost in the country—angry at the roles
we were trying to become, angry at our selves
too small to be or reject them (so the large
ghosts waited, armed, at the limits where our sight
failed, out the night door)—we kept asking the songs
to tell us about change. When were they too long, dwindling
down hillslope distance?

                            When R. D. Laing
lectured on Jefferson's Lawn, the newer young ones drew us,
in their protest leaflet, with tangled snakes for hair
and Picasso slippage, double nose and eyes . . .
And what they wanted as the woodblock Jesus,
square beard and brow, square and blunt even the line
between Him and His Star; to whom "the Rapture"
meant the day that we, the Lost, would seek them

room to room and street to street, learning too late
the God they served had snatched them bodily out
of all this, before letting loose the fire . . .
Then Janis: "Oh Lord won't you buy me
a Mercedes Benz"—her scrawny voice an angel's
unaccompanied trumpet—
                        & the world slept in Ulro.

Twenty years, Leonard Cohen . . . New sounds in the street: the dog
strangled in mid-yelp that means that someone's
turned off a car alarm. Soft ringing
of an early-shopping cart, picking up bottles
before the recycling van.
                        New viruses, early cancers
the price perhaps for the antibiotic nimbus
of childhoods where no friends died, that let us carry
our young looks so fresh and far into middle age . . .

> *I saw a beggar leaning on his wooden crutch,*
> *He said to me,* You must not ask for so much,
> *And a pretty woman leaning in her darkened door,*
> *She cried to me,* Hey why not ask for more?

Shapeshifter voice, yearning and shrugging off—
insight that should hold and kill, gone down the flood—
I would step twice in the eternal river, if I could,
with you, with Suzanne, with William Blake of Lambeth,
where every atom lives, the most fleeting love is answered,
every moment is fire, each singe an opening eye;
and still think it's my fault, if, at the great concert-fairs,
I never quite linked up, but always ended watching
on the ragged pathways out of afternoon
the dust give back its odd, quizzical stare.

After the Election, 1984

That glop on the window—you could call it heavy rain—
on the night ride in *Silkwood,* when Meryl Streep is telling
how her marriage just happened, abandoning her children
also just happened—and then she begins to sing
Amazing Grace that saved a wretch like me
and the camera moves outside, her face barely there through the rippling . . .
It makes me think of how we don't have last names
in public anymore; how we do so much of our shopping
to music; or the statisticians deciding
how far Reagan must praise peace, and Mondale war.
They interrupted the returns for the "Hallowe'en murderer," trim
and moustached like his captors. The wind was high,
or they were tugging him along so rapidly, through the wide
concrete spaces, but I think he said "I regret it," rather tonelessly,
not an admission, like the announcers regretting
how their East Coast projections affect the West Coast polls.
When Silkwood goes to die, she sings it again, in sunlight,
that becomes the light in the rearview mirror, pursuing,
haloing her hair; and the voice-over continues,
'Twas grace that taught my heart to fear . . .
It's the last we see of her, but something seems changed,
tenser, clearer in the air, though we know that nothing
will ever be proved; the company will buy off
the relatives with a settlement; a scriptwriter will remember
something heard in college about martyrs
or the Aztecs: their blood goes back, to refresh the sun.

Speakers from the Ice

When your hand touches a cold enough piece of metal,
it's your hand that gets torn.

                      —The ice that becomes your flesh
is gray, wide, smoky; lost in it
as on the smoky shoulders of a highway
that crosses into too many other highways,
or when the TV crosses into electric snow
and you've slid too far inside it, on the bland
announcervoices, to come back anyplace
shining with solidness—you might find yourself saying,
"When he took you, why didn't they stop the highways?"

And a voice might answer, in that cloudy   (abducted
slipping-space: "One moment it was my skateboard   child,
that wasn't, where it made sense; the next it was me.   1988)
The moments after—well, I suppose they've lived them
in their own way, drifting into my room, asking my toys
whether I lived or died. But they couldn't block the freeways,
the way you said—there are too many of us,
it would stop the traffic, even, to your door.
But it seeps back on all of you . . . My hours of happiness
aren't real now, even to me. My name is Horror."

"They'll never find you," you say. At that, the ice gets redder,
as with the blood of those who've torn their hands
free, in order to live; or as if a sightless city
ground its rusts around you. From that, another voice:

"Odd, isn't it—in our age it's the victims
who wander lost forever. Where will you find the damned?"

"Some acts have always drawn everyone to Hell,
even alive." Then, nagged by some lost headline
like a half-heard song, you add, "But don't I
       know you?"

And the silence saying you're right, you go on,   (vigilante,
"They weren't quite wrong, were they, to call you   1984)
       'gentle'?
'Machines don't hurt you,' you said, and talked to them
hours on end, soothing the least scratch of their unease
in an algebraic heaven. Was it waiting changed you,
the lonely crystal, the tetrahedron of planning?"

Then he: "You don't know. To do what everyone is thinking,
take that upon yourself. Ride in on your donkey,
idiots gawking from the trees. A whole restaurantful
paid my bill, when I came back, and felt so damned."

And you: "The city hated the smoky slippage,
which it called toleration. Of course, overcrowded prisons,
too-long dockets, even signs addressed
expressly to criminals—'This driver carries
no more than $5 in change'—are not precisely
toleration.

                But the city was on holiday
those December days, its Feast of Fools, its invisible
master bound at its feet."

                        "But waiting, too, for me
to trip myself, to pay for what they wanted.
The limping god, remember? *Who touches iron
is iron*. Why so many years unmarried
and fascinated with guns? Why the itchy calls to the neighbor?
Why shoot them in the back?"

                          "Could someone who'd rehearsed
as long as you had, ever have waited
to be really sure?"

                      "It was so far behind me,
so far in the past, when I actually saw it happen,
backs or fronts didn't exist. Of course I crippled
the least guilty—their obscene martyr."

"They were live flesh, too. There's more than one book about them—
the Projects, what it cost to walk down the street.
But it's you I fear for. I see you going down
the long path with its constant flashbulbs, their eerie metal
inextricably part of your veins . . .
Never to wake up and be just anyone.
Never not be part of floodlights and killing again."

And then you can hear the shrug inside his silence:
"Don't worry about me. There's much worse farther in."

And with that there's depth behind him, and a wind,
you don't know from where, but as if, beyond all warmth,
a thousand turbines blew it . . .

                                    Images. The little   (Lockerbie,
towns of the sky fall on the towns of earth.   Scotland,
A warehouse of burnt bits two inches long,   1988–89)
where someone, slow as a child, tries to explain
how it explains it. Thin nakednesses, moving   (Treblinka,
into a snow-screen; and, again, announcervoices.   1941)
There will you find the damned? Who only speak
to telephones—
        "The heroic execution
of Flight 103 . . ."
                —or the wires, stretching   (former death camp
from the sound truck in the grim suburb (the   guard, *Shoah*)
    filmmaker
sick with numbers, sure that no promises
hold, this far down)—
                "Fur diese arme Leute   ("For these poor
war es sehr, sehr kalt"   people, it was
                          The sneaked-in camera   very, very
catches the emptied features . . .   cold")
                               And the wind . . .

La Pastorela

Like the first centuries. The outsiders get wind of
what's at the center, down thousands of desert miles—
the golden Empire, pulsating, tossing out
its tentacles, leaching their strength—and wanting so much
at once to share and despise it, break it down.
(Bomb-factories in New Jersey; slave-ships foundering offshore . . .)

But these are different. Their language held this place,
right for the dust-glint of olives, the waterless flame
that, from April onwards, licks across the hills
like an Inquisitor's, centuries before
they were brought here in truckloads, seasonal, the flat hot fields
another country the American highway
looks away from, like Europe from the cattle-cars.
But for ten years my mother and her friends have come
across the hills from Carmel only Arabs
and movie stars could build in now, to see them
take the old Mission for their new-old play.
And one year it even got on television:
the shepherd-girl dreaming St. Michael—Linda Ronstadt
come in shopping-mall-rainbow jewels, solar gauze,
out of the too-white California sky
to send them out on the roads to seek the Child.
The journey long as history, the eternal
gray of the ghost-sloughs, hill oaks scrubbed with winter.

The Hells Angels roaring through Hollister are remembered
in the spiked leather wristbands
the demons wear; Manson and his girls in *El Cosmico* . . .

In the campfire songs at twilight, the devil joins in,
as when does he not, on such journeys?
 They've got him splendidly,
as he is, a subtle fellow; offering no
kingdoms or orgies, he gets people to see things
a little wrong, out of the steady balance
of wants and limits.
 (In our multicultural
English Departments, you can hear him whisper
to the ethnic poet, the postcolonial critic,
"If they fault a line, or question a fact, it's racism;
they've been having *their* say a thousand years"—
then tell the whites, "Look how sloppy they are, how arrogant;
always getting something for nothing—that's their game.")

So he turns them all to sheep, and sends them running.

. . . In the real church, of course it's better: the Shepherd's staves
bright with crepe paper, tin cans, lanterns, feathers, flowers.
San Miguel by the altar; Lucifer at Hell-mouth
(draped over the church door); and the girl kneeling
where their rays converge . . . Lucifer (Luzbel) and Satanas
are two separate persons; Satanas is androgynous;
at Armageddon, St. Michael and Luzbel sweep in
on high-necked wooden horses, black, star-blue.
The angels bullfight the little devils, the ones whose horns
keep slipping off; then the great protagonists,
swordless, fling *brujo* magic from their palms.

At last all draws toward the altar; resonance
of whitewash on Roman arches; a real baby;
gift-giving; and the Hermit does a dance,
because he owns nothing to give. Then they file back,
an angel and a devil, two by two,
and, walking out, we shake the actors' hands.

Out into America, under the thick, full stars . . .
Does it help us accept it all? Our human lights,
thicker than stars, over what was once plain country;
a culture of quotation marks, without boundaries . . .
"When we first came," my mother says, "it was all Mexicans
and five of us; now it's the other way round."

      Accept, even, Linda Ronstadt
saying to the Devil, in her version
of biblical English, "Rise, you horrendous beast!"
—though perhaps in a thousand years some hybrid flower,
lovely with possibility as French
or Italian, will bloom out of the wreckage . . .

In the film, the shepherd girl wakes up, and finds she's
just a girl from the town; it was the scruffy old Hermit
knocked the eagle-lectern down on her head when he mounted
the pulpit; and suddenly
she was no longer watching, she was part of the play.
And she'll be different, now that she's been there
at the manger in Bethlehem, with the real Child:
in love with a young field hand, who's come in
to be one of the actors; sorry she blamed her mother
for going on having babies and keeping them poor . . .

A little north of here, someone slightly younger
didn't wake up; she was found thrown
in a scrub-wood by the highway, outside Cloverdale,
by a man let loose after serving half his sentence.
By all the bad childhoods, sealed in blue tattoos
like Satanas' wristbands? By a society
that won't believe its own moral judgments sixteen years' worth?
By the gladiatorial murders on TV?

How short a time back, we were the severe Republic,
gone back to filch learning—but also keep our distance—
from the sly old centaurs under the olive trees.
Now the sex-shops in Milan are called "Magic California."
If you were with Tacitus, and walking in
that brick market-labyrinth-arcade, near the Forum
of Trajan, where the terror
of its having happened over and over can be felt more
than in Circus or Colosseum,
what vision could you have truer than the moment
when the Devil holds up the crown of thorns on fire,
and shows (in the high-tech version) the whole future
flickering within: Calvary, the long procession
aslant the hill-ridge, like the one Death leads
in Bergman's *Seventh Seal;* the sponge, the spear;
and says, in effect, "You'll be poor all your lives,
miss out on the fun of America, for *this*?"
And though we know it's a false question: they'll be poor
anyway; the corporations
have paid for this broadcast, as Augustus
was "always a good-humored spectator" at the Games—
still, how we're gladdened by the countervoice

that says, so strongly it needn't be out loud,
out of the center of that flaring ring,
it has always been so; says, *if you want your life
to mean something more than its moment, go through here.*

Mansard Dreams

The hairy Magdalen. Your love of the emptiness. Your old lovers.
(A clacking at dawn, and the old woman calling
the pigeons, a belch of soot, to a higher mansard.)
Your dream that I'm small, in a cage, and won't eat anything
you cook me, however delicate. My dream you're a tiny dot, dancing
and your voice from somewhere else: "You can always step on it."

We wake to Paris, the long flights down, the gray.

Fine-flanged, almost heatless bedroom radiator
we had to unplug to use the one in the bathroom
without rousing the *interrompteur.*
Madame Plans, the half-Spanish concierge. The plumber-handyman,
his office his kitchen table—the door banged into it—
troisieme etage. We were on the fifth, a narrower
spidery turn below the unimaginable sixth
where the crone lived.

            We came out one day and found her
blown into a corner like newsprint, spitting a mutter
we didn't know was addressed to us until Madame Plans,
sweeping two flights below, said *Ils sonts gentils.*
Va t'en, ferme ta gueule.
After that she'd knock at the door, when I was out,
and ask you why I did that, tap-tap-tap on the pipes,
driving her mad . . . We thought, the typewriter? But no:

I did it specially,
it seemed, between five and six in the morning.

In the shadowy side-aisle, the wooden Magdalen waited for you,
your talisman, her cascading
thicket rounding and hiding her whole body
to the knees—like ascesis, or a woman's lust
as seen by a man . . .
      I remembered how you climbed
a tree once, beyond where I dared, and I saw your flesh
sinewed on air and the light give of branches,
suddenly free; and I thought, *she isn't like that
on land*, or should it be, *my nerves won't let her?*

Year I literally drew a box around my head
to shut out things you would say.

Year you couldn't feel we were really *here*
unless you saw it all, say, in a bus's
side-view mirror . . .

And when we broke to the streets, that Easter evening,
after working all day at being here and happy, cooking
blanquette de veau, it was like breaking prison.
I could hardly believe we'd get to the next lamp globe
in its mantilla-net of new, broad leaves
still leaning on the splendor, before it spread
too wide, in the dark waters . . .

We couldn't grasp it, somehow; now even the hot smell
of the Metro makes me happy . . .

By the end of the year, the crone knocked when you were out.
She'd made a discovery: *C'est votre femme qui fait ca?*
The plumber stopped answering calls. He just sat at that table
day after day. In April, he was dead.
Did he kill himself? Was it cancer? Would we have known
if my French were better, if we weren't such—*mice*!
Mansard dreams . . . Did Braque learn something from
the slight inward angle their zinc takes from the straight
wall plummeting?
Einstein says we needn't grieve, being a whole, divided
by the illusion of time. Dogen says in that dimension
you have a sixteen-foot body, solid gold.

Linda Does My Horoscope

For Linda Wing

"*Poets . . . think about fate often if not obsessively.*"
—Charles Baxter

"Let's not *talk* about *my* life, but the Vikings won.
It's a big deal here. In fact, I timed our call—"
"For after the game?" "*And* after the phone calls.
I've never seen a chart with so many retros."
(Retrograde planets, that from earth's perspective
seem to stop in their tracks, and then move backwards.
Ice-masses, recalcitrant, like the heavy atoms . . .)
"Retros mean . . . challenges. They can be opportunities.
You don't get things done the way people think they should be."

"Of course, we're not quite sure this chart is right,
if it was War Time—" Permanent Daylight Savings,
part of Prehistory, like transport planes
slowly thrumming over . . . I didn't ask my mother,
I was too embarrassed; besides, I have the feeling
I did once, and the answer was confusing.
"My hunch, knowing you, is that it *is*."

Explanations: intercepted sign, trine, ascendant . . .
The afternoon lengthens, cloudy in both cities,
both alone in our houses . . . I have—
I've had it many times—an odd
clairvoyance of my birth-hour, winter, cloudy, darkening—
not *in* the hospital, but the streets around it—
and a special hush, like . . . I'm afraid, like *Christmas* . . .

"It's an Aquarian's nature to be hopeful.
An air-sign: gets places by flying. Genius, truth-sayer,
exile. Your Sun and Moon are close—
Sun's your core essence, Moon your emotional needs—
that's good, they like each other. But, Moon in Capricorn—"

"Not great?"
            "No-o. 'Watch out, they want blood,'
this commentator says, but she's an Aries,
they don't trust earth-signs. My mother's a Moon in Capricorn,
it's not all bad. Let's see what someone else says.
'Black-dog depressions' " "Yes." " 'Deep need for love,
but guarded, paranoid. Not afraid of work.' "
Yes, yes. The years in Arlington, nothing published,
bleakness like antimatter, and wifely silence
palpable, past the study door . . .
"Capricorn moons *accomplish,* even if slowly.
It's a sea-goat, can go anywhere—swim, climb mountains . . .
They're tougher than they look, and do not lose."

"In the seventh house, all this has to do with marriage.
You like weird people—Aquarians do—
but nothing works without the intellectual connection.
Most of all you *need* a mate—though, lacking that,
a best friend will do. You'll spoil people with attention,

charming, but frightening in your dependence . . ."
B. Three weeks, no letter. N.
"Men with Moon in seven devastate women,
they're smart, and soft, and listen, listen, listen.
Placid appearance, inside hysterical—
heart on springs, reacting to how *she* reacts . . ."
Indeed, indeed.

        "Now we come to planets.
Neptune's in Libra, but retro. Your mystical side
develops late, but will help your writing."
Sitting zazen on the stone at MacDowell, forty-three . . .
"Venus in Sagittarius, which she doesn't like,
another hint that love's going to be trouble—
freedom and commitment . . . Nothing at all
in the ninth house, and there should be. It
has to do with ultimate reputation."

So maybe this *isn't* the right chart? Or . . . a blank.

Eleventh house. Gemini. "This is the big one,
ready? You've got a *stellium* here—
three of your big planets, two of them retro,
two asteroids. Mars and Uranus
are closer still, a conjunction." (The Christmas Star?)
"Mars is your boy-planet, drive, combativeness, sparkle,
it's happy in Gemini, and likes Aquarians.
But Saturn, Uranus . . ." They come, the antimatter,
black-hole gravity, majestic, walking backwards,
that sucked years eerily
in, back, or down . . . "Shyness, inhibition."
Nontenure, nonpublication, hinterlands . . .
"Uranus—well, he's called the rude awakener."

Yes, yes. That sense of *meant to be*
that in hindsight, anyway, reconciles mortals
to almost anything.

                    "Pallas near Mars
is auspicious, though—she likes war.
Here's where your Capricorn persistence comes in,
your Aquarian power to grow by leaps.
Trines, too, indicate a happy outcome."

"Trines are good, squares bad?" "Don't say that, I'm all squares."

More explanations. I scribble restlessly.
Two hours, my phone bill, on *astrology*!
And yet . . . I half-see them, Pallas and Mars,
swords drawn, like Walsungs, among the heavy atoms
that want blood . . .
                      My mother
once said, you *smiled* so much, as a little boy.
For a moment, my two understandings—
the charmed life, the afflicted life—
come closer than they ever have, a *stellium*.

"Thank you, Linda—you've taken such *trouble*." "You're welcome.
Leos, like me, are lucky for you, but nuts.
Everything in opposition teaches."

It must be almost dark, where you are, already,
like that blessed hour . . . "Time for soup.
I hope I haven't scared you. With those planets,
you wouldn't be alive still if you hadn't
somehow learned from it, and gotten through."

Puccini Dying

I could not find the music
that would marry
the hero to the ice-princess in this life.

Her music came easy: mirror-shock, avalanche
of desire and pride retreating
to the inner cave: sleep that perfumes the world . . .
And the other's, the slave girl's,
who stands for
flesh and devotion, and must be sacrificed.

And *his* voice, that believes it could persuade anything.

. . . It was perhaps the one time I really *wasn't* guilty.
We really were just having a cigarette together
at the foot of the stairs
after late cleaning-up, and late scribbling.
But my wife threw her out; went and talked to the priest;
screamed *whore* when they met in the public street.

Her family sued; barricaded themselves in their house;
I fled to Paris. Then Doria
swallowed a corrosive
and took five days to die.
The doctors examined the body, and pronounced her *virgo intacta*.

I said I would never live with Elvira again
after that. But I did. Perhaps
I needed to look in the earth's stony mirror
to know myself . . . Perhaps
I was too much at home with executioners.

The Prince of Persia goes by, and the moon rises;
his head is shown. Liu goes off, draped over
a little Tartar horse, like an old figurine,
and the old king follows . . .

Next month
they will take me to Brussels, make a hole in my throat,
and stick seven radium needles in the cancer.

My secret was simple: to circle a note, above, then below,
stands for longing,
the way people will sit and watch wave after wave at the shore.

Now there is a man who says
you must not repeat a note
until every note in the whole scale has been sounded.
They are driving me to Firenze, in my new Lancia,
to hear him. Perhaps he
and the blind old king will lead me
into the toneless *night that has no morning.*

In Paradiso, speriamo bene

(in memory of Peter Taylor, and of Robert Lowell)

1.

Between space, as I often am
in dreams, in some precise, geographical way—
one unreal street, or structure, between two real ones—
Charlottesville this time, north from the University,
suddenly you're with me, pointing out a shop window
with birds, all raptors, stuffed on dusty perches.
Their plumage mottles, dead-white to leaf-brown
to iron filings . . .

Waking, I understand: it was your generation,
the giants in the earth, who knew "the good
is the enemy of the best," and ranked the poets,
ranked their lines, even; drank till three or four,
and again at noon, and if the waiter heard them
mutter, "I really shouldn't," and turned around,
drawled majestically, "You weren't supposed to hear that . . ."

And all the more, as they grew older,
bewildered by the facade of days and buildings
no argument resolves;

each hangover breaking more blood vessels, memory-links;
the smile afloat on the body two-thirds water;
after three strokes, two decades of insulin
in public bathrooms
(delighted when a black man misunderstood, and grinned)
saying to death, "I've too many books to write . . ."

—*Present moment! That sad hero,*
who dies as soon as he's raised his sword and slain
all of his fathers . . . How can we live it,
knowing its guilt, and knowing
how infinitely far it's already left behind?

2.

But you showed me something else—the little vials
like Jewish Jahrzeit candles,
rosy wax sloshed and melted up their sides
over half-obliterated scripture.

You said they were poems; asked if I could say them
from memory . . .

Instead, a story: perhaps you told it to me
the first time; now, it's in his biography—

Cal was in Venice, at the Basilica
of the Frari. He wanted to see the Titian.

But his friend, angry with him
for not noticing the Madonna
a shaft of light picked out of three centuries,

because it was by *ignoto,*
told him, find it yourself.
Even he, he had to guess.

It's hard to miss: in fact, he'd described it
in a poem, long ago,
the red robes flying, "gorgeous as a jungle bird";

but he stopped a passing monk.
(One has to know, here: he botched languages
so badly, once in Paris he was given
the special seat for *mutilés de guerre*.)

Dov'è Tiziano? he asked. (Where is Titian?)

To which the monk, his finger pointing upwards:
In Paradiso, speriamo bene.

(In Paradise, we have to hope.)

Caitlin: A Biography

The wild white hair in your ears making you look
like a baleful owl; the frail, belligerent eyes
like some gray poet—Baudelaire, in the etching—
affronted by Time, Old Age, Death and the World.
Your low-slung, widening waddle, from behind
is like what animal? Skunk? Raccoon? A *badger*!
—A badger's, too, your sudden bite.

Later, your head comes knocking against my elbow;
half-averted, your sorrowful, affectionate gaze . . .

We're none of us responsible
for our childhoods. Wild kitten from Lake Temescal,
found starving by the rangers who had your mother spayed . . .
Your thirteenth year, I sit beside you and say, "I knew you
when you were a bundle of fleas. Anne wanted
to send you back to be fumigated." (*Snarl*.)
"But 'all beings by nature are Buddha.' " (And, slowly, *purr*.)

Of course, Anne *felt* the bites; E. and I didn't—
easy for us to moralize! So you lived
six months alone in the "activity room,"
the storeroom, really . . . Let loose in the morning,
you'd lie in ambush for the smallest of us
to venture down the stairs.

                              The divorce meant
five houses for you, too. And then the one
that made you an indoor cat again brought also
the Interloper, that ridiculous miniature,
Yellow, endlessly friendly, endlessly curious eyes.
Clear enough, to you: she hadn't a *soul*; you did.

(Whatever one is. What Christian ever measured
his hopes for a second life
by the similitude of your eyes, ears, nose and brain?
Hindus gave you a second chance. Buddhists, "All beings"
etc. notwithstanding, shrewder: you
the only animal that refused to come,
when Shakyamuni was dying, to say goodbye.)

Perhaps a soul is this: a small refraction
of the great shadows moving us from above,
a knowing more than one knows—one block of Berkeley,
interrupted by rooms in Evanston, in Vermont . . .
This much I'll say: you are
a person; you can purr and growl at once.
Mnnrao, you complain
("Crying *What I do is me: for that I came*")
out of your daylong slumber on my bed.

Dinosaurs

(after the PBS series)

At the far end of an upstairs wing, and scarier
for the way the long hall darkened toward its midpoint,
just where the ribcage rounded overhead
and the neckbones began their climb. Of course he couldn't
come alive; but if he did? On the high walls
strange waters, limber palms, filled out his world,
and the huge haunches, gray and thick as *Sinclair*
motor oil, crunched them down. Surfacing through time,
more bones, and dioramas. By the exit
a sabertooth has trapped itself
chasing a glyptodont into a tar-pit.

And Como Bluff, "Graveyard of the Dinosaurs"—
Highway 30 still two-lane—whose gloomy profile,
more than the sign, made me drag my parents into
a wind-silvered, raw-board shack, to buy ribbed bits of
something wilder, even, than being there, on that road.
I missed it, this year, on I-80; now the TV
confirms it, and the two scientists who fought over it,
the one who died first bequeathing his skull
to a museum, just to prove his brain was bigger.

We thought *their* brains were too small; that's why they died—
and depending too much on the extra one, in the tail.
Now it's not so clear. Between their age
and the start of ours, there's a thin layer of marl—
the same in a dozen countries—with *glass*
in it, and outer-space minerals, and metal droplets
thinning like the crest-ring from a splash in milk;
which made them start looking for the great rock that's shown here
wheeling in from space, rough and so brilliant
it dissolves to a ray of dots, a computer-map.
Then the globe shawls itself in fire.

Strange, in ten years to have learned a way of doom
we never thought of, when we thought of everything—
plague, nuclear winter, the Son come in His Glory.
And always out there . . . One dazzled over western
Colorado, a few years back, then swung up, missing
earth and the headlines.
                        And hardly less
strange, the millions of years that didn't need us,
our kind of mind. The huge herds of
Triceratops, like bison, roaming the endless plains,
that wouldn't, of course, be *Triceratops*
for sixty million more years. Shall we say, they had Buddha-nature?
Did the rock, whirling from space, have Buddha-nature?

Why do we smile, then, to know such things existed,
ran gracefully, even, over the face of the planet,
its new face we'll never see? With the first flowers
upon it, to scatter their quick alphabet
before the slow teeth, used to palms.

If the rock wheels on us from beyond the night,
what I'd wish for is that something, somewhere,
half-guess your lineaments and find them lovable,
as I find the animator's duckbills, lifting
their placid heads to watch the big thing lowering
bright, then darker, behind the bands of cloud.

After "Death of a Porn Queen": Traveling the Great Basin

Everyone wants to sleep with a girl from a small town.
No one wants to be a girl from a small town,
facing the choices—waitress, wife, switchboard girl.
A difficulty of Being, and its elsewheres.
So the beautiful ones—boys, too—move on, and play themselves
in huge light, if they're lucky; if not, a hotel bedroom.
And those left behind carry the heaviness
of the body, the dingy hallway
where no one cleans the paint-drips off the Western mural.

Towns with their white initials on the hills,
towns that still seem an echo of the mountains,
plangent, purple at sunset, rock of another planet
over the far-off cat's-eye of the trains . . .
But no one wants to end in the graveyard at Winnemucca,
unfenced, no hedge even, gravel, a few low trees,
the statues' glare like junked cars—a part of the lift to the ranges . . .

Red Cloud

                     The cat
had to come into restaurants. She was too rare,
there were "catnappers." So your parka went down over
the carrying-case, like a parrot's silence-cloth,
and you gripped the handle through it, hoped the waitress
kept her eyes up, on me.
                            It worked, oddly—she knew
when not to mew—except one off-hour dinner . . .

In between, sharp Abyssinian ears
back and forth in the rearview mirror.

                *

Power plant past Reno, with four white blinkers
on the tallest stack to warn low-flying planes;
and then the hills fold down . . . always the gateway
to the earlier country where slow freights stretch out
a mile or two in the Sinks; where gypsum chutes
rise through openwork toward rust-iron roofs . . .
Rock Springs where you wrote down a conversation
between two bullet-heads, in the Chinese
railroad-car diner, and the cat kept quiet:
"horseflies in Texas—stung the cattle to death—
but you could drown them in oildrums filled with beer—"
"AIDS—should stay in Africa—they started it . . ."

You said, too, one night, "We never talk, just argue"—
my travel nerves, bad as my father's—

*

To Cather, transplanted from Virginia,
an erasure of personality . . . the roads
petering out in bunch grass, land *bare as a piece of sheet iron.*
When a lark flew up, she couldn't stop herself crying.
All her life she feared going back, even drowsing off
in a cornfield, in case she happened to die there.
But when *the country and I had it out*, she was *gripped
with a passion I have never shaken.*

                            *The writer
fades away into the land and people of his heart.
He dies of love only to be born again.*

*

We're here. Bald brick of the one-crossroads town—
our one pause, in your five-day rush home to school—
with little Romanesque or Arab zigzags
out of the brick itself, or out of red stone,
or white capstones on the windows—Dr. Archie's
second-story office, we've found it, there's a plaque—
and the turreted, townhouse-size bank, the "Cather Museum" . . .
You compose your pictures, your first way of focusing
on anything at all, this summer . . .

The streets themselves cobbled with brick. In the background, always,
the flat hot sky . . . as if it were a law that the soul
has to feed on what is most unlike it; that creation

begins in erasure—not just this place, but all Being
slipping past the horizon a block away.

*

Upstairs was *ours*, the children said. No grown-up
ever came up there—the unplaned beams and rafters,
the siblings' cots, and then the nook she finally
made wholly her own, with the red-and-brown-rose wallpaper . . .
She dragged her bed to the window, hot summer nights
she'd rather have been out walking—*as if her heart were spreading
all over the desert . . . vibrating with
excitement, as a machine vibrates with speed.*

You especially want to photograph that dimness,
but it's too strong in the end—the roses indistinguishable
from old tears in the paper . . .

*In reality, life rushes
from within, not without. There is no work so beautiful
it was not once all contained in some youthful body, trembling.*

*

The soul has to learn about cruelty.
                    Vivisection,
her "favorite amusement"; her high school speech in praise of it
still framed, in the bank, past the old-fashioned teller's
brass bars . . .

            The old doctor
took the girl on his rounds in the buggy, let her give
the chloroform once.

After that . . . to be inside
another being's skin, actually *see* the blood flow past . . .

Was it shadow-revenge, outrush of power
in one who'd lost so much? (Biographers tell us
a boy once threatened to cut off her hand.)

Or an indecency native to art?

—A taste, at any rate, she eventually
gave the worst man she ever invented,
then gave him her loveliest woman.

*

Towards sundown. The trackless "Cather Prairie"
just before the sign on the empty road says "Kansas";
but we don't get far in its messy, spiky tangles . . .
Why still so vivid?

                I was losing the power
to read your face, its doughiness, its charm
more opaque, this puberty summer—fearing each bad moment,
each dinner I was silent through, or snappish,
might become permanent . . .

                    And already enough
sense of destiny a kind of iron clenches
in your voice when you say, "It's so hard to be good at anything,
good so it matters . . ."

                  But still, this twilight,
by the locked Depot—you wandering, taking pictures

from the weeds, the disused spurs—there's such peace in the air
I might be your age again, or She
still holding it all—the stationmaster's chair
sealed up, fifty years?—in her vast, impersonal eye . . .

Three bows, down to the dirt, palms lifted over
my head
          I won't make here, but two months later,
by her grave in the icicle warps of crisp New England
fall morning light . . .

The world is bare as a piece of sheet iron. And no work
was not once contained in some youthful body, trembling.

from **PRESENCE (1983)**

Friends Who Have Failed

They leave from positions of strength, like all baroque
civilizations; leave the statues we cannot imagine moving
for heaviness caught in the skirts . . .
We watch their gestures grow finer and more nervous
in the widening air.
They are the best judges of wine; talk always at the glittering edges
of things, the terrible auras . . . The afternoons in their houses
hang upside down, like objects seen through wine.
Their footfalls die an inch away in the carpet.

And leaving, we wonder why the world
has not appreciated this fineness; why clumsier juggling
finds favor in its slow eye . . .
But we have not understood the world; how its way
is to destroy without destroying, the way air
levels a mountain; things fly apart in a vacuum . . .
It wears us to the hard thing we cannot help being;
and if the only hard thing is our determination
not to be hard, it wears us down to that.

For Robinson Jeffers

More and more I think about you, and the others—
your likes and unlikes—who chose to harden their difference
until it was so dense, it would shine of itself in the dark;
lived narrow into towers, to the faces of wives and children
loved more steadily than most; turned their even-planed desks to the ocean;
and built the beds they would die in into the stonework
of their hand-made houses, trying to care as little
for fame as the dead, or hawks . . .

        Oh, I know
all one might say: that what you fled and resented
was the father within; or, worse, some incapacity
you half-knew in yourself, and could not cure;
that the more your peace was accomplished, the harder a spectral
humanity seethed from behind the planted forest,
from the cities as you dreamed them . . . till the love of yourself you began with
half-recoiled at the self it had made . . .

And yet . . . to become something simply
because one can imagine it, and it isn't there;
to say—as I half-hear you—*the others have chosen*
to elaborate the surface, until it seems to them they
are surface merely—a celluloid barely tingeing
the blank face of the streets; or else they name themselves

*stones and roots, without eyes. What have they left us
even to wish for?* And then, returning: *those
who hated me did so not for my faults, but because
I wished to walk out of myself in a soul and a body.*

House-Moving from Tournon to Besançon

Stéphane Mallarmé; Fall 1866–Spring 1867

for Bradford Cook

It's an awesome thing, when fate takes you at your word
at eighteen or twenty. *If Dreams weren't greater than Action . . .*
Happiness on this earth! One has to be pretty vulgar
to stoop to it. When I wrote that, two months
before marriage, Marie's weak chest
seemed a kind of grace-note—the blood-hearted snowdrop—
sharpening the wild-thing poignance of her eyes . . .
And *un*happiness? A curtain-line, a fling of the sleeve.
Not, at any rate, this matter of two fatigues
grinding each other; the worry when the child
gives her slight cough; the bone-cold rooms,
and happy, sometimes, for those . . .
                            Our move here was as moving
is—one's old chair in the fall rain an hour
because the men want coffee . . . The irksome part was the need
to be composed through it all; the need, after Tournon,
to think about stopping rumors before they start.

(I must tell you they fired me in mid-term. Wads,
with spit in the middle; and their parents complained of *me*.

Shoving my face forward into that brute
heaving, making it say *he loves*—
like teaching an atom to be a molecule . . .)

The moral: prompt visits
in order of rank; sincere show of interest; cards.

The town? It could hardly be less designed to lighten
such burdens: another of these ancient centers
of war and religion; drip unabsorbable; gargoyles—
The worst, though, is always God: the blank stone staring
west into nothing but its justice, as if
He were as stunned as we to have awakened . . .

Empty nets of matter; that thought our surface-glitter
was something . . .

*

      How eagerly I waited, that first week, for life—
my only real one—to compose itself
with the room as I have it: midnight; the mirror; the window
bulged with my Dreams like firelight—like the bottomless
drawer of an old chest . . . But when I sat there, feeling
the words reach to name, then deaden on the page's
familiar virgin emptiness—the thoughts
that returned on me! Ah, my friend,
if, after these gods and ages, the realization
of all our thinking is to think itself Nothing,
why not be the truth?
                            I grew unable to feel
myself there except as a kind of skin on the thinness
of the always singular instant. Can it hide itself

in the folds of the curtain, will it run to join childhood
in the mirror-waters? I tore the drawers, for a trace
of it, of *me* . . . And the things stayed, in absolute presence,
inviting me to complete their thought with a stroke
swift, unrevisable, perfect . . .
       I floated downward
in the un-being I glimpsed there (I can't
put this plainer—but, even in class, I lost the meaning
of the commonest words); yet half-wished it now, desiring
that every Dream should die, and—stiff and white,
as at dawn, as from the waters of that old story—the poem
of the world float free.

      One day—gray and almost spring—
I looked in my Venetian mirror and saw the person
I had forgotten. When I say I still
need to see him there, to edge
to the next word, or thought—you will know how far I became
Nothing; or simply a gift the impersonal universe
has for thinking its causeless Idea,
our Work, the great equation
that cancels at last.
    I have seen the ends of more than
one life; and have hardly the strength to lift my hand.

        *

More negotiating with fools, not to spend another winter
in this terrible place. They have denied me
the Département of Lozère, unaware that my work denies them
Paradise.
   I must say the two seem much
the same to me now, watching the first green shiver

along our pollarded plane-trees. I remember how the heat
exerted itself on things . . . A half-witted shepherd
was on trial for rape. The mind moved, behind blinds,
with the sure drift of a sleepwalker: hearing my Faun
hesitantly raise one note to the next, then flow—
and off the fountain-glitter came the nymphs
of living space and air . . .
                         I felt myself twang half-
inside things: even the hard-cased scorpions that made me
keep the bed legs sitting in cans of live gasoline.

And if one thinks the world, in that reverberation,
as if Spirit were making it, what difference?
I am trying to learn
to think that way again; not just on the squeaky
first string of the brain. On Easter, I got a terrible headache
from brain-work alone. By an enormous effort
I braced my whole chest-box, seized the impression, and rang
it inward and downward. Ever since then, when I truly
create, I am gone except for my hand and a heart
enormously hollowed and beating . . .
                                  And nothing
is named now: the object
goes by in the miracle of a vibratory
near-disappearance . . .
                     into what—air, God? Who will ever know?

I need rest after all this; more rest, perhaps,
than kings are ever given. But you are not to worry;
I can't tell you the weight of peace it adds, to have taken
the future up in one's hands. I see
one book, or two, the years fallen into their crystal.
I can't think anything will have been much amiss,

if God send my old age a pleasant actress
willing to have visits in the long late afternoons.
I won't even mind much, if both her windows
and mine look out onto long railroad yards.

A Progress of the Soul

In the beginning there are your limbs crossing simply
as the beams cross in the summer cottage ceiling
—pine-soap smell from the bath—

and there is a story, that goes as many ways
as the cobwebs in the corner. In it, the dead get married
as often as they get baptized in Brigham Young's
Temple, and through the same medium, our pale bodies.
Before you have pubic hair you see the gown
Grandmaman is willing to your bride; you must cherish forever
an invitation to your mother's wedding . . .
O the legions of names that will never have faces, the cancers
that grew on them, as if they were the faces . . .
And the young sit uneasily, stiffly as wood, at the point
that the threads all somehow insist on coming back to.

But the young have intangible allies: the senses
waiting to blossom like deep horns into the skull
and open the echoing valleys; so the outside
arrives in a thunderous surf. One day a lilac
sprig sways, and you are shaken from head to foot with the vertigo
of *why here and now go on at all*, when you blink your eyes.
Then the bad old story is over, and the poem
begins, that goes nowhere, but only deepens and glows.

        Have you felt this? the school rocked
        to the roots, the floors weird planes and sliding—
        the gulf of the future
        that hides in bones, turning
        all first loves' faces to statuary . . .
        the love of the thought of your thought made
        of green cells . . .

But how sluggish the blaze looks to those who are still in the story!
The boy who slouches, one leg tossed high over
the chair-arm, and answers with hateful over-politeness,
his mind on negligees far as foam on the beaches of China,
seems hardly alive . . . As they try, so they think, to reach him
with their barbed remarks; as they go on trying, his anger
fogs their lives with the deathliness they see in his.
O the endless summer coastal fog
of the photo they live in! the Fourth-of-July lights worming
the cataracts of my blind grandmother's eyes!

        So that, years later, the flashes
        catch at you oddly: was it really your great-
        grandmother who died dragged
        by a riding horse through the Bois de Boulogne?
        and her husband, the gentle
        composer, Ferdinand de Croze, who pined
        away and died within a year
        after leading Grandmaman
        through the ice caves up Monte Rosa?

And then you know you will live in a bare white room,
its splendors books and the covers of books, and tiptoe
against all that entangles you back and smaller—the musty
taste of cabbage, small flocks
listed in the chinks of the nomad rug—unless
you can imagine what is nowhere now, can make
the black dots of the photo flush with dots of rose.

For My Grandfather

F. A. Bächer, 1874–1968

We were putting our shears away after trimming cypress
at the end of August, when the coast goes clear and dry
to the level light,
when I tried to convince him by the medieval proofs:
that nothing happens without a cause, and so
the causes must rest somewhere, in God . . .
He wouldn't stop asking, "But what causes God?" And then,
still chuckling, but moved, "No, the universe
goes on forever, but we have finite minds;
our minds aren't made so as to understand that . . . "

I resisted the infidel, that goes
without saying; but something started
in spite of me, at the dignity of his thought:
how he set his own mind
                        beside itself,
as a useful tool, to increase immensity;
as he laid his garden gloves near him, on the stone wall—
each crinkle
              ridged in the even, magnifying light from which
the evening star would, in an hour, sharpen—

and set himself down beside them, saying "Oop-a-la."

Trois Gymnopédies

for my father, George Williamson, 1898–1968

My father requested that "Trois Gymnopédies" by Erik Satie be the only music played at his funeral. The italicized couplets in *Dark Ages* come from a fictional morris-dance in the mystery novel *Death of a Fool*, by Ngaio Marsh; other thefts are from Huizinga, Donne, and my father's essay "The Libertine Donne."

THE PACIFIC GROVE GRAVEYARD

If the Judgment never comes to alter
your quarrels, Father, possibly the foghorn
will do as well, deep-thrumming
through the two hundred yards
of sand to your grave.
Like a severer violin,
I would say, if you had liked them.

Once you taught me to know
its voice from the quarrel-
voices of old seals
rounding under my sleep.

Now the shy deer come and crop
the memorial chrysanthemums
clean to the wrists of stems.
        How often
you tiptoed over the floors
of the house you designed with your own
hands, and that never stopped booming,
to howl at them,
      as they nibbled
frail "natives" in the moonlight fog.

DARK AGES

When I think of you I think
of the outmoded ages: the Iron Crown
of the Lombards; processions and
bells; the slow and exact punishments,
the barbarous, tearful reunions;
         and especially
what Huizinga mentions, the absolute
separation of day from night.

 It is not just that I stood
before the small gate to Duke Humphrey's library,
and saw the cloudy, waxy leather rise
to the heraldic rooftree,
your heaven, gained
by your shy illuminator's awe, that I
stand outside, barred
by the cruder presumptions that have made me, me.

As from before a great fire
your face emerges, dancing
   in its old shame,
driving your Aunt Amanda
to church behind the thousand-farting drayhorse;
red, bulbous, elf-light, Swedish,
the rawest
and finest face I have yet seen on this earth,

Mr. Peanut and the old dill pickle,
and little Eheu,
and "Think, think, thou wast made in a sink"
as you scurried, half-naked, into the warm kitchen . . .

   Once for a looker and all must agree
   If I bashes the looking glass so I'll go free

But your face darkens like a mountainside,
"Honor thy father and mother,"
and wanders off all day to read
in wounded, important displeasure.

And I and my friends appear, chanting
the names of our devils: Shit
   the First, Fuck the First,
   Mannerhater the Great,
and dream of the island where we are four kings
and the parents are kept in dungeons.

I see the long gray country rope you once
lashed me with,
for shaking it at you
when you called me a crybaby.

Then, nothing . . . rain-light . . . sad breath
as though still climbing the long stairs
of Chicago . . .
                  One winter in Kansas
you were measured for a Christmas overcoat
and thought it was for your coffin.
On the last day, you wished to be taken from the hospital
and thrown by the side of the road.

   Here comes the rappers to send me to bed
   They'll rapper my head off and then I'll be dead

But I can never get
around the crooked corners of your smile.

ARRANGEMENTS

Choosing the coffin,
unfinished redwood,
                searching
the plasterboard record-stores of Monterey
for the one music, Erik
Satie's *Trois Gymnopédies,*

                      telling
the distinguished guests to stay away;
                          leaving my father,

where he taught me to know
a landscape not to the heart's liking,
no image of its peace, but cypress
tightened to the shape of wind

                              but you loved it, singing
"My little gray home in the West," as you pulled down the driveway.

                                  *

In the year of the Crash, when Hart Crane
fought his parents for the strength of an instant's writing,
you gave half your salary to yours,
gave up your poetry,
and waited (fifteen years)
                         to have a child.

But set out gaily to be death on feeling
unfused with intellect
                       off to gay/gray London,
you and Mama schemed to give each other
a first edition of Lord Rochester,
long watched, with anxious pricing, in its window
                          shadowed by the British Museum.

Were your twenties lighter-spirited than mine?

In your essay I at last sit reading,
you three years dead,
you argue that John Donne
"may not have violated his own integrity"
if, on "plumbing the emotional depth of that
inconstancy" that first so pleased him

  So flowes her face, and thine eyes, neither now
  That Saint, nor Pilgrime

—an invisible darkening, a moon eclipsed, reason's pale taper
more windblown—
                        he turned to the single Light.

After one operation, you went back
to Camp-Meeting terrors: Hell
a great ring of heat pressing you down,
                              afraid
it might graze the hems of those who stood by
robed in mysterious coolness.

But you died the modern way, knowing
the strength of your disease, but not its name,
with no preachers or Bibles, but your peculiar God,
and the tiny bright-horned marble bull I brought you
from Crete, I don't know why . . .
                          You angered Mama
by your habit of only sleeping sideways,
your hand closed on the bed's steel guard-rail;
you apologized, saying
"I've spent so many nights in hospitals
I began to feel it was friendly."

And later, open-armed
for the last cardiogram,
ringed with wife, son, an outer sphere of nurses,
you said, "My faithful people,"
your eyes dark violets
like a farm boy's the first
time he thinks a girl likes him.

                Carmel, September 1968/Charlottesville, December 1971

If, on Your First Love's Wedding Day

If, on your first love's wedding day, your roommate's
locked up with the phone (which you need) and his girl
while his ex-girl sleeps on the living room sofa, homeless;
at nine, Miss Now departs; Miss Then at ten
ascends to the first-best bed; you wait in outrage
muttering Hart Crane; then she walks through your room in her slip
and doesn't see you enough to know she's teasing . . .
what do you do? Untangle the phone from the bedclothes,
and dial, your right hand sloshing gin "Here's t'Clara"

And if, when you're back, alone, calling all friends,
it's Miss Ex who drives you to the liquor store;
when the clerk doesn't know you, won't take your I.D.,
she flares up on your side, "Why, he's almost a professor!"
You come back, top down, high on gratitude,
while horse-chestnuts cast their red-prickled flowers before you
on the hood, your hair, as once with Clara driving . . .
And so, when she leaves the party suddenly, you
follow, and find her in tears, having at last
placed a call to her parents (missionaries, Baptist).
What do you say? You say, "My first love got married
today," if you're drunk enough.

Dream Without End

to the memory of Joel Sunderman

Was sie mir wollen? leise soll ich des Unrechts
Anschein abtun, der ihrer Geister
reine Bewegung manchmal ein wenig behindert.
—Rilke

I

I have dreamed it again, the day that you come back,
Bruce, Dick, Charlie, all of us gathered somewhere in Ohio,
Bolt upright all night in a hotel room furnished only
With a square walnut table, then filing downstairs at dawn
As your Rolls Royce pulls up like an exiled Ukrainian Count's, a hand
Sticks out, a Pope's, with rings; then . . . Joel, death has been good to you,
You're so fat you can't stand, and wrinkles cover your eyes.

II

Walking the East Village streets in hungry cold
While our filmmaker host went to Hasidic heaven on grass,
Came back to say World's End Two Years Away
(Two years whose end you didn't see),

A week before you fled
The Good Doctor, your German father, to Berlin,
We tried to thrash it out . . . your hard-won Marxism
("Nobody should have to be a hat-check girl")
Against my lapsed-Christian martyrology—
Henry James heroines, and mad John Clare,
And how Shelley outlived his death by writing it . . .
In sympathy in fear,
We talked through the night from our pallets,
Hearing in time to our voices
The plumbing cough, and down
The numbing distance of our legs
The seconds, clicking, dive . . .

And then walked out next morning into air unwarmed
By the sun though it turned the skyscrapers to mica,
And saw a child set out before us
Thrusting his shadow before him like a sword,
Trailing, then dropping a mitten . . .
A spiffy career girl in a steel-gray coat
Swerved in mid-stride
To run and return it, patting the ear-muffed head.
"They say New York is such a cold place," you said;
"But I see things like this happen all the time."

Next day,
We passed her in the same block at the same second.
She looked through us like glass.
But when I glanced over you were glancing back,
And we stomped into Bickford's, clapping our iceblock hands.

III

I remember other girls, soundlessly laughing
On the highest platforms of the fire escapes
In pullovers, combing
Their tin-blonde hair to a jet stream . . .

Then Haverford,
Our homecoming:
Cake-white in the same cold snap, our professor's house riding
The frosting like a microcosmic toy,
With the healthy groan of the hearth-fires, and thick sleeping-
Bags tossed for us on the sleeping-porch . . .
       But Bobby,
Hurt by improvisations on his poetry,
Asked me why it was I kept away from women,
And was I really queer?
     His wooden face kept coming
In pain, between
The sips of Isabel's protective vodka . . .

Then dared me to prove my manhood at a party.
Streets swam, undertowed with drink and rage.
I paced myself through wrought-up stories
About gay actor friends . . . brashly kissed
An old friend's fiancée good-night
(Acts that reversed themselves, popped "queer" or "straight"
Into my brain like colors in roulette)
Until my feet, somewhere, were shuffled
To cool wind, at the center.

Between the dorms and the house was a thin neck
Of woodland. Summer or winter,

Pissing into the blackest shrubs, or running
All the cold clearings while one breath turned to frost,
It frightened: the place of trial
Between private pain and the created home.

That night, we assayed it together.
Arms locked to shoulders, we inched down the hand-
Rail of the iced, log stairs,
Melted in mud, refrozen at crazy angles
Above the fast night road.
I pulled you down like an anchor; we broke, spun wide.
I could feel the road-ice lifting me like a tide
To the gold tangles of sleep,
The light-bulb moon
Ending the long corridors in my repeated dream
Of helpless sleeplessness . . .
      The car
That came after to check on our safety nearly hit us.

I would thank, now, their skidding kindness; and thank Alfred,
My host, who came quietly in and unlaced my shoes
When I had laid me in full suit
Out cold, on his cold porch;
And, before all, thank Joel

Who said, next day, to Bobby,
"You could have said all that just as well of me,"
And was told, "That's obvious; but I'd never want to."

This, after I brought you "home";
My feeling, not yours, that it was kinder, saner
For you to come say goodbye.

IV

Our exhausted goodbye in 30th Street Station:
Our tossed-down, splay valises
Braced back the rush hour like spokes of a wheel
While I made my childish last demand
That you steal pages from the filmmaker's "Memoir"
Retelling (comically) my love
For a girl he wasn't able to make, either.
We both pretended
Your silent bob meant a sincere "yes,"
Because the train started to move . . .
You clutched the black briefcase to your breast and leapt,
As if you died, for my eyes, in that second . . .

In dreams, you let me know I can still write you
And it is only at the mailbox, trying to write down a Zip Code,
That I suddenly break into tears.

V

You too, like Shelley, wrote your death,
In the class yearbook, of the class suicide: "Sophomores,
We learned that we could ride the Paoli Local,
Or let it ride us."
We thought you merely callous,
Though you had shown us your father's music room, the carved
Rococo *memento moris*
In Latin, German, Portuguese, and Bunyan—
Under which star
He ruled his string quartets of fled Ukrainians
And bullied your mother straining at the keyboard.

*

Your whole life a child's bad Sunday,
In which you sought
The elation of crowds, rare stamps, an elegant style
As the child turns to dominoes and parcheesi . . .

And even these slow friends failed you:
Burning your frail novels
As hostages into the darkness of his will,
The last coin sold at a song
For passage to Lenin, West Berlin, willed silence . . .
"He has to have sold it," your father
Said: "There was no other way."

Gog-eyed with glasses, joints wound up like clocks,
A tiny bow at every second word . . .
Yet had to fall for the fastest girls, and sorrow
At the Piero face on the centerfold of *Playboy*;
After three failures,
You took to asking Alfred's young daughter
To prowl, with you, your fabulous antique bookstores.

Did the spiffy girl turn and start running
Down those unearthly, now, two years
(The light-years going from her eyes like glass)
To leave you something simple as a mitten
And life, set right, in your hands?

You went loveless, but came back
(Because we failed you?) love
Given over
To Caesar and slain.

You ended, for us, the unproductive pain
Of youth;
We were all the profiteers of your death.

VI

We grow by drawing inward. In our
Successes, you are wasted: Alfred's daughter with Dick; these poems
Cut from your life, but truer to you than your own.

As you, too, turned from us—"some residual fascist
Instinct for final solutions"—the one Berlin letter . . .

But it was *No Season For Tears*, when Isabel's
Eyes sparkled against the plush funeral, the family
Circling inward, the mother's ghost-spoken eulogy
Misquoting that, your best and cruelest story.
"At least there were ten of us there who really loved him!"—
Words in which we seemed to walk forth, beyond falsification.

For two years, I could imagine no other end—
Into the lanes, the night-lights' tiara, the quincunx
Of the witches' wood . . . the great house itself melting
In its mirror-gleams, back to trees . . .
                                        Under a bough
We pause a moment; you ask me if I learned more
By staying to the end; and are, as you once were, patient
For my life; for my answer, as it once was, fervent
And undecided . . .
                     this year, missing in dreams,
A shape gone, and a darkness listening.

Bernini's Proserpine

I

It was the first time a really sumptuous girl had taken his hand,
and Rome lay before them: the Spanish

Steps' Cinderella night-piece, dream-whitecaps
falling/rising to Bernini's drowning, monstrous boat . . .

They left behind his more glamorous, her more dowdy, friend,
"transvestites like everyone here at this hour,

only which is the boy, do you think?" "Or which is the girl?"
then burst to a run, now close, now arms' length, leaping

three steps at a time, eluding
Americans and more secretive wayfarers,

until they broke at the fountain's inner rim, and stooping
to drink, he saw

through the fine iris of the jet, her hand
furl slightly, a stone shell;

and knew, somehow, that she would hug herself
through the next block, not entirely because

of the catfight in the blackness under a velvety
Rolls Royce, and the one that ran out, its stomach torn . . .

They met the next day for sightseeing, but their talk
had grown distant, though voluble; the other couple

quarreled; and, at last, she stood him up . . .
But they met once more, and because

he was in love, they were somehow
together again; and at the end,

almost as a gift, she told him the story
half-there from the start: how she was picked up,

in Florence, by a distinguished-looking man, who said
he was a millionaire leather-store owner;

was separated from her friend, and then
—not raped, but forced

to do something perverted, at knifepoint,
in a pine wood, faintly lit from an outdoor night club, near Florence.

The man returned her to her hotel, and said that he loved her,
and that he would kill her if she tried to leave.

She left, in any case,
by the earliest train, not asking for help; but was frightened

in crowds; and after—she puts this impersonally—"I couldn't
like the thought of sex, not even a boy holding my hand."

*

And the first time he comes back to Rome, with his fiancée,
she wakes up screaming . . .

"I dreamed you were sitting naked, except for a loincloth,
in a fancy bar; and you said, 'When I was married . . .'

I said, 'You were married? You never told me.'
You raised your martini and smiled, 'Oh yes, in college;

it only lasted a few days. My parents
had it annulled. I was very young.'

I said, 'You never *told* me,' and suddenly
there was broken glass around, and I started to scream . . ."

He shivers, because he *has* never told her; and walking
to the washstand, his hangover dreadful, he mumbles

"Sometimes not even aspirin does much for small
Sienese paintings" (sinus headaches)

not even in—his first letter home—"a city
where one is never out of the sound of water."

II

That the oldest city grew
                        around that moment's knowledge
(never exactly known, a hundred times imagined):
                                      the centuries' breath

gone out in a single night from the pockmarked stone,
at the unknown hour when the water
                                      is dead in the deep tanks,
in the mouths of men
                   with the mouths of snakes and birds speaking
out the backs of their skulls . . .

                      After their last meeting, all night
when he tries to doze, touches pour
                      over the stone Proserpine of her body;
he sees himself draw a sword, and plunge it
                    into the soft underbelly of Death;
and at last, when he knows he will not sleep,
                          his bones
rise light as to Judgment, confessing
            their wish to dance naked with the shattered husks
of arches . . .
                            Morning comes
as if it were an endless plain, with laundresses
                    on the roof of it, singing
like Tosca's shepherd, some
unplaceable

                  Io de' sospiri

That the city lives around you
gone
     with your long stride, coarse tongue, and Holly-
                                wood eyes,
thrilled in the *son et lumière*
when they turned the Forum pink with Caesar's blood,
and really mad at my mocking . . .

                          You were sure
that Fanny Brawne was not good enough for Keats; but likely
to go home to your first lover, a young doctor
who didn't read; you thought a man
was always wrong to let a woman know her power
over him . . .

        So serious about being
so ordinary, with the sumptuous
assurance of your body: the American
sexualized innocence,
                      demanding, submitting,
demanding to submit
with innocent right to the thousand strengths and prices
of men, harsh and lavish *Fortuna*

                                —the World
come with flowing, tanned stride to the city that is
the World!
                  but with the ghost
of a pursuer . . .

I have imagined him as a stone, fixed in place
in a city whose only flowers are stones,
through which the heat comes and goes fiercely, on which the light
falls poor and yellow at night
                        for continuous wearing;
the sad, dry will of the Medici craftsman against
Fortuna . . .
                as if he wanted to leave in you a language
of stones, of dry heat and wearing,
against that impregnable innocence, adoring
and unable to stand what you were . . .

                              for what common rapist
expects a date the next night with his victim?

So that he enters my language, that would have raised you
with it
          in useless love, useless revenge, and the sainthood
of the bones rising . . .

Nothing I knew in you could have prepared you; and yet
you were alone with your story, and told no one;
and ran for the earliest train;
                              met me,
tested yourself on me; were shaken,
a little, in your plan for your life; and changed
my dryness with your listening
so that, after ten years, the poem flows never
from my loss, but your weakness and courage

                              Daphne's laurel
rushing, ramifying space around the
                              penis of the young
scarcely awakened god . . .

a wandering touch in the ages of the city

              as if it were an endless plain, with laundresses
on the roof of it, singing . . .

O fountain mouth, thou giving one, thou mouth.

Aubade, Reconstructed in Tranquility

That June, you ritually sent me home to sleep.
When I looked back, only the reed curtains

Waved in your suddenly darkened window. Rows
Of glass lab stairwells loomed down the block toward home.

I liked to compare their night-lights
To timed photographs of the sun rising;

But the real sun crept around to north-northeast,
Where the early freight

Whistled near as a bird-call in the next tree.
Yet the light rose equally, from no direction;

Porch-slats shone like sculpture. I entered
To a single yawp from my pacing cat, and fed her.

Dumb to record all this, dumb to show you
A face not formalized by incomprehensions . . .

Now I towsle your head to wake you in full sunlight,
Yet our days seem to meditate on the hour

That no steps bring me back to, that I can even imagine
Happening to others, and not quite make the connection.

C., Again

I (BRYN MAWR, 1961)

When your feet went always naked,
tap-tapping to the Fifties rock,

it was cars leaving
for darkest America, the muscle roads, the beaches

arriving in strange wind. It froze me to your armchair,
tragic . . . and turned you elfin-angry, asking

me if, in my novel, you slept with your home-town boyfriend?
and what should one think of Castro?

You had a divorced grandmother, her drunk cousin slept too near the fire;
a dead mother in love

with Thomas Wolfe, and you liked blond boys with angry cars.
A brass cross from Provincetown, set among fan shells . . .

When your eyes widened, what spring.
Nothing will show me again its wild-skied, uncertain

lift in early March: your ordinary perfume,
the hills sinuous on our walks, the sound of rivulets

ending nowhere and nowhere, reaching the sea in the ear;
the sweet, sudden graveyard where I bragged of atheism . . .

Our day is ending; we go out to the diner,
old bus chrome,

the only place you let me buy you dinner.
I call myself desperate; lift hands toward your cold-kindly face,

in the green, in the neon, the haze of too much looking,
the pure oval of an old photo:

if I could leap through, I'd be father of Protestant armies . . .
How many days to divorce?

II   (CHARLOTTESVILLE, 1970)

Since I have been here I have wanted
to write a poem for the football couples,
too late for the game, too early for seduction,
haunting the fields, or, when it's gray, the supermarkets
where my wife and I splurge on wines . . . Here, many
are tweedy and bloodshot already; but once, a girl
pirouettes, then stops, frightened at the reflections:
the linoleum, me, the wood wine-arbor, the window
to the heaven of ice creams . . .

O beautiful house of the dusk, and the potted meats stacked like choirs!

A weekend was something you would only go to
with boys who didn't care;
so I'm moved to know that these, too, play at couples,

as we in our shabby Penn Fruit, and pause, hushed,
as I did once, late, at the over-huge windows dim-lit
and the cash registers lonely as priests.

Two boys catch each other down telescoped aisles, and razz.

You laughed like that, like a boy.
You wore a false ring; you piled our basket with everything
that was young and useless, cake-candles, love-comics,
and were not sold. How could I have understood?
I wanted Rimbaud, the day on fire, the iron
streets smashed like glass in the dawn of our first touch.

Spring Trains

In spring one notices the trains more,
in their unaging childhood:
the rust-red boxcars, the blue-black coal scuttles on wheels,
stopped a long time, then imperceptibly moving
through the new green lash
of the willows . . .

I think they will go by the windows of lonely peaked houses
where someone smudged and beautiful
draws one hair back over the seashell of her ear;
and I think they go to the night I once woke to,
dark peaks swinging from side to side of the sky,
and the rapids beneath shades paler than the snow,
while the Mormon evangelist wheezed in the next chair;
and sometimes I think they go to a secret mountain
in the center of West Virginia,
made of coal so black it is everywhere a mirror,
and you never know the moment of passing through.

Customs of the Barbarians

Paolo Uccello's *Saint George*

It is two children, and their pet.
The girl leads by a silk thread; her free hand
lifts, as to say, "how gentle."
The boy is the tin woodman of Oz. He sets
a spear like a pointer into the full eye,
so the blood flows down the fang and tongue of the cry
and settles on the ground, like a thick carpet.

While the tail, chartreuse corkscrew, rips for heaven
beyond the caves of the moon . . .

*

Some nights, when he strayed near the door,
he could feel the shape of the cold
killer, mirroring; the hand
reach for the knob, as his . . .

his set the lock.
Then, climbing up on the high white bed, wedged
exactly in the corner of the house,
and brushing her cheek, he thought
of their blood risen to spatter their own walls,
and he wondered what the chairs
did with their long night of useless possession.

He dreamed of missed trains, uncertain plans, long hours
spent holding hands, motionless
with his student, who is a great building of light.
While she went to school to the bearded lady,
and often overslept, perversely wishing
for her bad girlhood back, the room
whose address nobody knew, the dictionary
of an unknown tongue open across her knee . . .

But she cried and cried when he spoke of other women.

Her study door was always closed, his always open,
but they never, never
read a word of each other till the last black comma set.

They knew the star-chart, the bird-book, the wine book, the Second Volume
of Julia Child, and the sorrow
of the turtle with the bad eye, stacked in the dime-store tank.

They preferred to make love
in the first afternoon, when the sun, just slipped
into the tallest pine,
cast gold planes they thought their bodies would step onto
out of their clothes.

But they always fought at midnight,
slowly and painstakingly
putting on
the hard heat of the fox, the blue arms of the statue,
voices
ripping the ghost attics,
while the rooms filled
slowly with the ash-crystal of weeping,

and they lay
like broken puzzle-pieces,
like small beasts in the great cave of their bodies,
until morning could find the calm children of the picture . . .

They hung it up, when the bad years were over.

Last Autumn in Charlottesville

As we live, the years stretch farther on less feeling,
without linking down to earth,
like the bright-legged spiders that startled us
our first fall here,
building over such immense reaches of air . . .

                                            We grew to wait,
each year, for their webs
to catch our eye, out of the first clarifying tingle
of morning cold—like crystal-lines in the air.

Will we dream of them, when we leave here?
Or what will fill this space?
Something must tell us
we have lived six years, not handed everything
to the delirium-of-the-depths of time.

Perhaps I will remember the clean pinyness
of the house, when it was still all there to furnish,
even the night-echoes too sparkling to scare us . . .

Or how we stayed a few days into Christmas vacation,
with downtown almost silent, dwarfed
under its radio tower,
and came home one night to find

not a light on in our whole neighborhood;
how we hesitated on the doorstep, watching our trees
throwing their black points
around the strangely lightened and pearly sky.

Heaven

Cottonwood: boats of white thread
going, it seems, nowhere,
carrying a seed invisible
as the soul of Pharaoh, among the little servants . . .

I remember how, in such a week
dividing spring from summer
—a desert leatheriness on the June leaves—
coming home from church, I tried to imagine heaven

and got as far as a sense of pattern
before and after life,
its stained glass slightly tilted
to the summer air:

the old waiting for completion as the young
wait to know of the flesh;
somewhere, at each moment, an eye of breaking vessels
meets an eye that does not hold a single name.

Things the houses talk of,
with their smooth lintels, their unblinking eyes.
The spaces between the stars
that contain us, though none of us will ever go there.
The ephemerids holding it all in their one day.

And then, this was lost; for years I thought of time
as a series of lonely, brightly-lit rooms,
each a little different,
but with no ladders up or down into
layers of other life . . .

But the first time we wrongly thought that you were pregnant,
I heard a voice in a dream
saying, "We are going to the power station";
and I looked down, ecstatic, from a mountaintop,
at a russet brick building, grilled but windowless,
smokestacks rising among great elms;

and then I dreamed we were on a train, all windows,
heading into the lights of a coastal city,
and someone said, "You will be on this train forever."

I woke up feeling that I had been in heaven.

Childless Couple

Now the spaces open to them:
one friend instantly dead; one gone in misunderstanding
and resentments . . .
There are none to replace them;
and the girl students' faces are no longer glass.
It's like something—wheels—reversing; it's
the far side of the moon.

He thinks: *I've never taught better, been more instantly
sure of myself, when I write*;
and there's no lie in that.

She talks of a garden; they talk, too much, of their money.

When they walk
together, they settle themselves in all the houses
that have odd nooks, oval stair-windows,
or pointy, unexpected further floors.
Houses deep as money, as long gardens,
as the grandfather stillness of the wavy glass . . .

And the children's things
bracketed in the high dark, busy and stagy . . .
Once he saw the child's hat hung on the wall, like a picture.

How much is done to make us believe the world wants us,
when only we could
think of wanting, not just things, but a world!

They were animals every year, but not until this one
small British bears, well-behaved, with insides possibly
excelsior: Wuff and Padd.
As if growing heavy and woolly would call something
from beyond the sky to feel welcome, give them their names . . .

What? They don't know, any more; and the winter is ending.

And the dead friend, and the friend grown hostile,
tiptoe back down the years, removing
things small and unnoticeable, as if the firelight
paled, a minute, on all those tight-drawn circles . . .

"Did it really, Wuff?" "No, Padd . . ."

And the spaces open to them, the music
of the far side, that nothing
will catch back into any circle;
that is oneself continuing, only sifted
a little eerily higher
passing the equal stars.

Van Gogh's Asylum

Here, the whitest roses
Learn the lesson that life is fire: the secret glassblower
Distends their petals, bids the small veins run
Red miles.
In the calm upland air, the cypresses
Bend with the tensile
Throat-muscles of swans.

A place to go mad or sane: as, moving
Before the self-portrait in the Jeu de Paume,
One sees the centering eye
Break into its different focus,
A swirl of paint, the green blindness
Of fish muscle in unlighted sea.

A place with a calm goodbye
For the sufferer: lines framed from the ledger,
Monsieur van Gogh est sorti guéri.

I feel the blunt legs
Of his bed reach down into the spinning,
The walls of his nights tighten
And press like a seed-pod to morning,
To days and the works thereof,

The works: the eye's never quite motiveless
Gift to the things of its death,
A breath taking in
And letting go

What is taken and goes, those stars
Shedding light in glass panes,
Cured, gone out,
Starting to die—

That earth flaring up, sun getting a chill—

Hello, goodbye.

Old Toys Come Back

for my daughter Elizabeth

As from before the ages they come forth,
wholly forgotten, wholly pleasing; stripped
of detail, as if meant for flight—this white wool "dog,"

homemade, smooth as a lancing seal, and awkwardly
arrow-like, on its four back-slanting legs;
these folk-art lambs on blue . . . Once here, they nag us

with what they have left behind them; say that soon
The New House in the Forest will come, its thin frame rising
in a clean stand of trees; and *Scuffy the Tugboat*

will slip the hand and come down, past falls and sawmills,
with the man in the polka-dot tie to reach and catch him
as he passes the tip of the farthest breakwater . . .

So you have come down, scarcely smiling yet, liable
always to doze off, with motion and the outdoors;
stranger than a log . . . How shall we know to love you,

if not instructed by what loved us before
we knew our face or name?—messengers at
the landfalls of presence, shape; with the washed smoothness

the Platonists say the chairs will have, in heaven.

New Poems: THE PATTERN MORE COMPLICATED

Theory of Evil

Wind-flap of black trash-bag on barbed wire near Dixon,
in November, when the hills are U.S. Army color,
makes me flash on a story, somewhere in Hardy or Jeffers,

about farmers crucifying a hawk: the wing-joints carefully
extended, like the plastic, to take the nails.
They accused it of poaching. A missing rabbit, a chicken.

They were big to it, big as the sky almost, but couldn't
make it know what they wished of it, bow down to their wills.
They must have felt, if only they hurt it enough . . .

There's an opposite error: to think creatures *with* agency
are simply the World, our persecutor. We couldn't drive
without some such assumption: if we thought of

each thing we adjust to in the lurching steel
obstacle-course, as a soul . . . (Jack Abbott, used to
the highway-ethics of prison, killed the counterman

who told him the toilet was "just for employees.")
Which is why we're a little embarrassed, ashamed even,
when the car that passes us is a friend, and waves . . .

A man goes to the State Fair with his family. He sees
a child trying to climb the step of a small carousel
that's about to start. The driver's back is turned.

Sparse palm-shadow, Valley heat. The man is recovering
from depression, the crowds are hard for him, though marvelous.
So his first thought is, why should *I*

be the one to have to notice?—a reaction
as senseless, and human, as nailing a hawk to a rail.
Luckily, the turning starts slowly, the child rolls back

unhurt; and then everyone screams. And the day, in balance,
helps his recovery. Chaos theory tells us
the cars, like his day, shift pattern every few miles—

patterns hawks could see, though we, in the midst, cannot.
But surely there are places desolate enough, ill luck
just gathers and stays there. Crossing into Mexico,

I saw the trash-plastic flutter across the desert
in flocks like birds, and beach against the cactus,
as if it homed from all over the world to a place where people

were poorer, more careless. Like a homing thought
or obsession. Indestructible substances. Nailed wings.
Things windblown through the mind, as ourselves, windblown,

might pass a car on fire at the side of the freeway
before we can think, *I should stop*, or even look back
in the mirror to persuade ourselves, *someone will*.

Adultery

It must be the idea of a listener
that explains the rush to the mailbox, the bottomless grief
when she can't reach the safe phone at the appointed hour;
that stands by her, shut in the bathroom with a querulous
child, whose sorrow reminds her so of the father's—
that every moment of this has a witness, a Companion,
there with her as if she stood beside herself
and so was a person again, as she was before
love somehow slipped her back into Family . . .

It's this lets them postpone the thought of sex, or even
hear stories about good, or forbidden, sex with others,
transparently as God could; lets her write
one day, conscientiously or guiltily,
"You think of me as a guide from another world,
wise and clear, because I'm outside the rules . . .
Actually I'm ordinary, vain, very narcissistic,
fickle, not very honest, not learned,
a scared rabbit, mostly"
                           —knowing
he won't believe a word of it, or, believing,
will think her very saying it dispels it
like morning dew . . .

        And even
if every jot of it seemed, in the end, fulfilled,
and they scarcely spoke to each other, surely occasionally
he would still feel this was the Great Love,
the one where your whole skin's turned inside out.

The Factory

Every few months still a dream
tries to set things right between us—
not how it ended, but the loss of the feeling
you had some inestimable inner treasure
you can now again bring me, despite the months
your talk seemed flat to me, your soul an absence,
and I only your most ingenious, relentless critic—

I think of the light-metal factory
you loved so, when it floated
out of the cold November fog
north from San Jose,
with a hundred miniature-minaret
smokestacks, so new and flimsy
I couldn't imagine anyone loving it, or hating . . .

Where the Hills Come Down Like a Lion's Paw on Summer

She'd rewritten her story. I didn't figure
much in it now, or as a means, not an end,
a miscalculation . . . But for me, the high bare hills—
especially that cut, where the power-lines soar out over emptiness—
still seemed the place where I had met with a god,
only a god could erase so much and leave so little . . .
(Though it could comfort, too—as if a blessing
rose from the white dust—when love returned, and hurt.)
I was careful who I took there; but once I took a friend—
a male friend—to whom something so bad happened, so early,
his very interest in the world strikes everyone as a triumph
of life itself . . .
                      It was late October's burnt-orange
before the rains. Coming back, we half-saw something glide
like a shadow over a hillcrest, a carnivore's
low-slung lope, not a deer's.
(There *were* lion warnings.) And then the couple pointing
to the slope behind us, *my* slope, and there they were,
six or eight, leaping twistily into the air
so the snout came down where the tail had been. *Not* lions,
perhaps wild dogs?
                    I'm not
especially brave by myself, but I'll usually follow
someone else who's brave. My friend was off, up the steep
half-track by the fence. They waited
till we were thirty yards away, just close enough

to establish they weren't giving ground, then trotted
over the skyline. But . . . *not* dogs, the ovoid
almost feline ears, yellow fur, the draggly tail . . .
And the curvetting dance? *Maybe they were hoping
to trick the ground squirrels,* my friend said; and ever after
the place seemed half to belong to another god, a god
of twistiness, of survival
under myriad forms.

The Cure of Longing

(for Ari)

When you got him and, because, like me, you like drama,
carried him in your open shirt three weeks
like the fox in the Spartan boy's cloak, or beloved John
at the Last Supper . . . it wasn't that people liked you
more for his sake, though that mattered;
or public penance, either. It was a way of saying
you were paying attention
to something in yourself, so you'd ask less of women—
your hair-trigger; your drowned look, lost in the first waters . . .
Like me, you were given the study
of their grief, so different-seeming from ours, so cruelly
not afraid of loss, but only of losing
themselves in us—their need
to say goodbye in doorways, when we would never refuse them
being part of the life in the upper room, made tea
served wine . . . So it's not entirely a matter
of blaming the pole for the lightning, though that surging
the body can't contain, till it straightens out the arm
with someone's face on the end, is part of what you're controlling, nursing
the milk teeth of this small need. When you had to leave him
all day, it was all right, till about six—
maybe with the first darkening in the air—

he'd run in circles for ten minutes. Then something calmed him,
made the empty carpet endurable. What was that floating element,
you asked, and couldn't stop being with him, for anyone,
though evening sieved, interminably, through the trees.

Martin Sloan

What is the thrill still rises through my belly
at your name? Do I think my early efforts
are *Shakespeare,* or something?
                              —whom I invented
out of James Dean and Playhouse '90s, soulful
over things like *Cottonwood Leaves*;
out of long evening suspensions, sudden vertigos
at a cigarette, a lilac bush, a coiling motor;
and out of my sense that if I more resembled
my friend Ted, wore t-shirts,
could drive, and drove fast, failed a course or two,
Karen might ask to come over in the evenings
instead of just whispering with me in Latin class . . .

(When I showed my mother the scene where "Cathy" does that,
her criticism—"She's chasing him!"—
like all her worldliness,
outside any framework I could deal with.)

You whose speech I could only
hear in the two-hour window
between tawny shadows—daylight's
released breath—and the glory
when the room darkened inward like a ruby,
the pen-track went almost invisible,
and my parents started to nag me about the lamp . . .

You who somehow connected me to everything—
the cottonwoods, the sky,
tough talk I shied away from in the corridors,
as well as the old movies on tv . . .

A famous analyst tries to distinguish
hysterical storytelling, which substitutes
for the experience we fear having in our bodies,
from the story that rises tangled with the *soma* . . .
Which—*who*—were you?

                        A cliché, yet a fullness
my life would manifest piecemeal, if at all,
for years to come . . . As for Ted, he became
(I'm serious) a Communist Party organizer,
vowing his life to that world of failure
our whole decade romanticized, nailing down success.

And I had a fantasy, too strange
(so I thought) to record, after I at last wrote "CURTAIN,"
that I lived by myself, but you
and your Cathy knelt down at my bedside every morning,
not as servants, rather extraordinary
friends thanking me, because I invented you
and gave you permission to love.

The Fever of Brother Barnabas

In the nights, in the rare hours
when his joints could rest comfortably on each other, he thought
of the crystal heavenly spheres. What held them

safely apart? Like all the monks, he was used
to the smells of his own body: *earth to earth*,
as the abbot told them. But the salt

almost sweet smell of his repeated night-sweats
disheartened him, as if the earth were showing
something it shouldn't: a salt-lick, the long mud cliffs

that fell off below the refectory . . . Really, of course,
there is no Brother Barnabas. There is an English professor
who sometimes, in the night, sees himself so,

though in the day he worries about the classes he'll miss,
can he save the term? His girlfriend says, *Don't fret
about that*, and brings him huge bags of good soup and juice,

but won't come in the house. (Brother Barnabas only
ate the foods he had liked as a small child, green grapes
and unfermented cider.) Recovering,

he has the courage to read a book about a man
who wanted to be lost, and didn't mind dying,
his self compacting to a black dot, smaller and smaller . . .

Dread is hard to name. He'd realized his cat was dying
when he woke from a nap and saw the hunch, the awkward
way she sucked in water . . . But "realized" isn't it:

his body and sight were stone. Oh, Brother Barnabas,
help us with that space; image of lostness and care,
out of your dark age of plague and burnings,

hold it a little apart; let it come near.

A Place

It doesn't really matter where it is.
Chickens get fed, that will be eaten later.
Dogs die from poisoned meat left in the woods
by the hunters whose gunshots echo early,
shrunken old men waiting for the songbirds
at the far end of the olive grove. Winter is real here,
the hearths well-built and enormous, telling of
well-being and exposure, in a very old way.
Wild boars root out the vipers, and the porcupines
are as big as dogs back home.

Enough has been said of the beauty, but the hills
do wear the sun on their shoulders, long before
it softens the ice, down here.
                                And I, for a while,
am almost no one, a well-dressed foreigner,
and something inside flows clear, from the dream-time.

Letter to a Dead Poet

I met you twice. The second time you were dying—
I didn't know that—and seemed upset
about an unanswered letter. It was because my wife
was too shy with reverence for you; which I couldn't say.

Now I'm not married, but seem to have inherited
someone from you, someone you wanted protected
even back then.
Was it because her world could go so still
at a robin's egg, or a flower? Because she sang
in the shower? Or her fretful sadness, even then?

Or just that she is beautiful, and was young?

Another poet said you had the slowest-moving mind
he'd ever seen. Sometimes her mind seems like that,
especially in quarrels. But both your minds went strange places.

She must, even then, have had the power
to make things whole (so seldom whole herself),
as, the morning after
her mother's sudden death (yes, Buford is gone),
she had to stick her toes into the Gulf
because that was what they did together;
the Gulf which, she later said, was *like a soul*.

In your Anghiari, she showed me
your lines where you love the spider, because her web
made the dust that blew all day
into beautiful ruins, and upheld them.

Our day there had no dust, but was much, much colder.

One night our classical radio played Salieri.
It was clear he loved the notes. They were full and slow,
not formula . . .   Too slow, perhaps?
And this the man only remembered for envying Mozart!
All three of us feared, and could love, failure.

You know Vallejo's stone: *I've snowed so much
so you could sleep, Georgette*—as if his life
was broken, in his solicitude for her,
moment by anxious moment, into skill
and sacrifice and softness,
and only then could she . . .

Some nights it plays over and over in my head,
J'ai tant neigé, to a slow tune like Salieri.
You might understand why.
It gets colder. It seems important to protect
whatever makes beautiful ruins, and can uphold them.

(Greve in Chianti, 2000)

At the Villa Serbelloni: 1998

The "Russian criminals," the Ukrainian
feminist called them. Actually, they were mayors
and scientists from the secret nuclear cities,
numbered, not named, until 1990; still
off the passenger routes, behind barbed wire.
Jeanne said, they *smell* like Russians. Huddled together,
smoke, alcohol, and vests. In the hallways,
always on cell phones. But when I said, "they're saying
'It costs more than I thought here, sell a bomb,' "
the Americans didn't laugh—the liaisons
from Brookings, Livermore . . . Think of a country
where half of the produce is backyard-grown,
but the Fail-Safe system may fail, on the missiles,
because they haven't solved the year-2000
computer glitch. How strange that
the silly Livermore Lab architect
should have said, "They're like the monks in the Dark Ages.
They want to pull the drawbridge up, and let the chaos
rage outside, so long as their learning gets handed down."
And the liberal from Brookings said, "We have to help them.
Only the ones who can make the bacteria know the cure."
And one of them told Tomasz, the Polish painter,
"I have done twelve operations without narcosis."
We thought he meant torture; he meant a marvellous
byproduct of fission, xenon gas.

—Where the full moon rose one night over the horn
of Leonardo's mountains; where I felt
the need to think about epic, so being human
could stand as an idea among the long
ideas, lake and mountain, herm and cypress;
where Tomasz painted the dog he hoped would meet him
on the other shore, paw just dimpling the waters,
and the architect said, "He got a *month* here
and only did three pictures. Why,
I paint two a day in my spare time!"

MLA Notes (1988)

for Joanne Feit Diehl

We agreed we could always spot us at a distance—
tweed-buffered, bemused
not consciously angry, out of place at street corners
as an armed statue, and unlike,
say, scientists—who've never
been told they aren't, or should be, sexy—somehow fussily
self-fondled at the edges . . .
                                 "What
kind of convention *is* this?," as the whore
said to you in the ladies' room . . .

Is it our uselessness, our failure
to be good at, say, machines; or a peculiar
second-handness toward life itself, gives our faces
that permanent aging childhood, that apologetic
arrogance around a void?

                          The very fluid
of life, passions, crises, imaginations,
how one thought hooks to the next—to which we add
nothing we stand behind, nothing that's purely ourselves—
coursing through us; and turned to no purpose, unless

making others love the same superfluous
quickening to the essence, is
a kind of turning . . .
                              Certain forms of magic
have always been handled by the epicene.

MLA Notes II (1998)

Of course, Pavese said it: "to hear people
    of the same profession,
trade, religion, sex, talking about it
among themselves, arouses disgust." And still, I'm back.
    On the BART crossing
under the bay, there was a man haranguing
everyone and no one. Hatred seemed
the impetus, to judge by the twist among the mouth-hairs,
though one could argue for energy, a ceaseless
    need to expel, discharge . . .

Everyone in this room would side with him
    (I thought), not with the mother
who kept her small son's wide alertness carefully
turned somewhere else—his head so blond it showed
    hers was once, *really*;
lourd et bourgeois to them, as the Frenchman said
by the subway exit . . . Arcana for ourselves, trash culture
for everyone else. Yet I'm here. Let's face it: power,
even small power, intoxicates, and gossip,
    and being mirrored; hotels

with their turning corridors are the image
    of the possible; young women
do shine, in their black suits and eagerness; this—

what to call it?—small whirlwind
    of molecules trying harder
no more or less real than the one out there where *death*
isn't a trope but something lurking
in the cold of the air, the welder's fire, the edges
of metal things; at some not too distant day
    quite unambiguous.

The Cost

You know the calls I mean. They come at mealtimes.
There's a dead machine-sound (while they check their list?),
then an accent, often, garbling your name.
I told one to fuck off, once. He'd said my name—
my *first* name—right, then added his own, a common one,
so I'd wondered a long instant if it was some friend
I wasn't recognizing. That was what got to me.
When he called back two minutes later, you've never heard
such a string of cusswords. "Bitch" was his favorite.
(Did he type me as effeminate? Was he black?)
I managed some reply, then threatened to trace the call
and sue his company, so he wouldn't call back.
He didn't. But how slowly the silence regathered,
with how many falterings . . .
Thud, thud, thud. My heartbeat has joined
the whole world I fought to keep out, car-whooshes, sirens.
And what of him? Would he track me down and kill me?
Such things have happened. More likely (I imagine,
ignorantly, doubtless contemptuously) hit his wife,
have one more beer than his limit, run a light . . .
We *know* the cost of swallowing anger, letting
the impersonal Thing have its way; but the cost of . . .
What was it Ahab said? *Strike through the mask.*

Moving Back to Charlottesville

Sometimes the ash-tree's cut off at half-height
though shoots strain higher; sometimes the screen door
hangs on one hinge, the kitchen free to looters.
Sometimes, on the other hand, it's all just right—
beautiful rugs, pictures and furniture
it took years to choose, have a right spot
among the others; and *right* was always *here* . . .

Is the unfinished business with your wife
as she was then? Or that first humiliation,
not being the University's wonder-boy?
Is it what you thought the middle-span of life
would be, and chafed at, now it's almost gone—
or you can see to when it will be gone—
suddenly reading itself as joy?

A joy you lived, or joy you squandered?
Shoots growing without the trunk; things that brought ill
because you didn't, and should have, locked the door?
Or a task brought to term? The dreams won't tell.
Whether bulldozers chew up the lawn
or you stand to welcome guests, by a lit fire—
something in you is always moving in.

Villanelle: For Anne

I had another journey I could not go
with you; or so I tried to understand
it, fearing I was greedy, selfish, slow.

For years it still seemed what was real was you,
in spite of the flimsy futures that I planned
when I said, there's another journey I must go.

The little meannesses I could not forego,
temptations to feel aggrieved I did not withstand,
seem not just selfish or greedy now, but *slow,*

as in slow-witted. Yet at last it's true,
beyond undoing, regret, or reprimand:
I have another journey I can go.

Why did both of us always seem to know
even our good years were pointed toward this end—
I was greedy enough, though I was slow—

there was "someone else." The night I told you so
and slept downstairs in the library, we shook hands.
I had another journey I could not go
with you; I was too greedy, or too slow.

Autumn Reparations

Rain seems to draw the smells from all the woods,
whether in trees or houses. Things hunch closer,
nearer the earth. Vegetables come from it,
crunched old-men's faces. Barbed and barbarous firewood.
Back east, shutters go up; and even here
people buy rugs and paintings for their houses,
more than they'd thought to spend. The opera starts,
dowagers put on their pearls and satin blouses.
(And some, each year, do not.) As if to speak
about recurrence, or praise-in-spite-of . . .   And the young
seem least at ease there, scrambled in suits
and low-backed dresses; though youthful passion
is what it all—down there in lenses and lights—comes back to.

Repair means both to fix and to go home,
or to a strong place. ("They repaired to the castle.")
Reparation, however, means making up to someone,
a new act taking the place of the old that set
the balance off. And cleansing, like first rain.
What are we making up to, with this season?—
the one we looked forward to most, as children,
with its feasts and demon-masks, and the cold shock
of apple-bobbing . . .

The Pattern More Complicated

I have my places, now, in every city.
The Wyndham Hotel. The Sutton Coffee Shop.
East Arlington. Cafe de la Mairie.
Circuits of habit, of self-comforting
for past desperation, of—meaning, even,
it takes half a lifetime's moving on
to lay down on the globe.

Arriving at the Wyndham, familiar soot-sting
of Midtown, some indeterminate change of season,
I set myself down and make my phone calls. I
am a man who sets himself down and makes his phone calls,
assuredly, though the bellboy has left the room.
Stiff lampshades watch me, and faded horsey pictures.
When I address the postcards to young women—
those I never had, those I lost in months or days—
I see their faces, not to see Someone
laughing, over my shoulder, at the List.

And most of them not born yet when—when—
                              I dream
often of the house in Haverford, now it's sold.
I drive past to look at it once more, but something—
sky-high windbreak woven against my gaze,
green, indestructible . . .

                    Before Dick and Marcia
moved out, new workmen, tearing up the kitchen,
discovered the wall of the old farmhouse, ending
at the pantry . . .
                    I keep thinking, we lost it, though I,
of course, had nothing to do with that divorce.
Like coffee stains on old fabric, heat-curdles on old wood,
it whispers, our generation can't keep things. They kept it,
Alfred and Isabel, whatever else they lost—
heart, lungs, esophagus; Alfred known at last
more for his dirty jokes and inappropriate
confidences, than anything else, except his parties . . .
But still a house in the old sense, grands seigneurs,
with a sweep of white newels down to the front door,
where we knocked, younglings, and were given sherry.

Jonny and I, and Dick, and Joel . . . I
could still walk that torn-up kitchen and find anything,
tumblers, tall stool to sit on, warmth-fields of several ghosts;
screen door, dog yapping to be let in or out.
Loss woven unnoticed into the whole pattern . . .

The last time I talked with Isabel, she could hardly
sit up at all, but we sat under the grape arbor
in the Eastern summer night—windless, stagnant, full—
and talked of how the dead go on, an ancestress' recipes,
family turns of voice . . . a thought ingrained in her
as the farmhouse walls embedded in the pantry's.
Trouble was, I'd known we'd have that conversation
as long ago, at least, as my early visits back.
It had nothing to do with just how much had gone wrong.
I loved her, but time had exhausted it,
too soon.

What do you do when you walk into
a new restaurant in San Francisco and meet C.,
whom you brought to that house in your mind, unseen companion,
since even (especially) impossible love makes
you see things twice, see for the absent other?
Thirty years. You don't recognize her,
her husband, the headmaster, recognizes you.
You're with a younger woman, it looks worse—
or better—than it is, but you can't explain.
She has multiple sclerosis. The beautiful proportion
of her eyes and nose is there, but contracted, somehow,
seen through the wrong end of the telescope.
Living in L.A. now. The headmaster's house
built for a short man, little squat pillars.
Finally started to write. Alone all day,
and the kids kept saying, "Mom, write that down!"
"What do you write about?" "Me. Don't you write about you?"
I'm sitting—the restaurant is so full—at her feet
on a small step, a posture
which seems oddly permanent—spring evening,
the two stone steps, the Haverford library . . .
And it's only when I get home I realize "Nancy,"
who died suddenly of an aneurism last year,
isn't the squat Nancy, the confidante,
but the wild one, with the dark glasses, the special car.

When I'm in the great house in Haverford, I'm lying
in bed, alone but thinking about the others . . .
One of my visits from Cambridge. It's early summer,
the room has no shades, I've never been anywhere
with so many birds, so all my thoughts are Eros,
that brimful Eros, straining through perfect images
like all the birdsong in the world, that start to vanish

after twenty-five . . .
Or it's at night, I've left the party early—
I can't stand, even then, to have such a hangover twice—
but sleep holds off, and I'm holding, reinterpreting
them all in my mind, as the timbres of their voices
drift from downstairs . . . I think I go back to this easily
because time seems already past, so infinitely
arrangeable . . . C. and I? Starting writing so late,
diffidently . . . not to have had to smash a marriage
to feel the brimfulness release, suffuse . . .
                                      Wherever
they went that night—friends, a hotel room—I so equally
wanted and didn't want her to stand apart where
rain stung a window . . . (Last scene of "The Dead.")

In my dreams the lost places grow enormous,
childhood apartments with tapestries for wallpaper
and chapel-alcoves, climbed to through ship's rigging;
or installations, worlds of airy fibre
that need to be thought in, and anchored, from outer space . . .
The vertigo Proust speaks of, the amazing
foreshortenings at the base. (Did Cal die
less than ten years after my father?)
But also his sense of a cathedral growing—
new shadows, amplitudes, as the arches close
and the fleche sharpens . . . (Did Jonny and I
address a multitude, ringing Buddhist bells?)

It's never quite mine, though—at best some enigmatic
ungiving other self's; or else I'm given
a little room to write in, off the kitchen.

The view out my window, at the Wyndham,
is like those archaeologies of my life,
strata whose lights and colorations are
unthinkable to each other. Men in yarmulkes
stand past dusk at long tables, tinkering small machines.
Mornings, one floor down, a secretary
bustles in with coffee and sits facing the airshaft,
by her potted plant. One day
the boss calls her out; she comes back and just sits there, glum.
I watch her not just because she's pretty, or reminds me
how my student once worked a job like that, in New York—
the delight of strange detail, and then the loneliness—
but something else, that for a moment makes
the "change" or "happiness" that was all we wanted, younger,
quite immaterial. Life, beyond my knowing.

Fantasia on some sentences from Combray

I enjoyed watching the glass jars which the village boys used to lower into the Vivonne to catch minnows, and which, filled by the stream, in which they in their turn were enclosed, at once "containers" whose transparent sides were like solidified water and "contents" plunged into a still larger container of liquid, flowing crystal

After the horror, it was the first thing I could let myself do that wasn't looking at the horror. I chose a moment when I felt a little calm, and made myself sit on the sofa until I had finished *Combray*. The book itself a container, gentle and crystalline, that permitted time to flow.

Days my country seemed like a parent, caught in an accident—for years you've only focused on the harm he's done . . . Now other things. (I dream I pull myself by burnt shrubs to the house in Monterey, and find my father there, still alive.)

Proust moved Combray halfway across France, so that it would not be spared the Great War.

It is because I believed in things and people while I walked along those paths that the things and people they made known to me are the only ones that I still take seriously and that still bring me joy

Tinny New York storefronts the firefighters pass, I passed in my courtship, passed three weeks ago—the city seeming so much safer than formerly, though an extraordinary number of otherwise professional-looking young women wore tattoos—on the way to an unpromising areaway, St. Marks Place, my daughter's debut in the Fringe Festival.

"Love of country," Eliot says, "begins as attachment to our own field of action."

And *Combray*? Because it too flows through everything? My grandmother's childhood, my self-exile, the years it shared my desire not to lose anything to time, and the years it shared a darker desire never to lose hold of something I called my "self"?

Literary? Eurocentric? So be it. *Never* . . .

Never, in the course of our walks along the Guermantes Way, were we able to penetrate as far as the source of the Vivonne

The quiet of no airplanes in the sky.

The pleasure of something equal to my life.

September 2001

Primrose Hill

Today the soft, usual fold of London sky,
threatening nothing.
Even to me, the dogs don't signify
danger or rage, a small one somersaulting

over the calm back of one slightly larger.
Paths crisscrossing toward a mild
summit, where you thought, *take the children sledding* . . .
A few things different, even in the weather,

you might have turned into any
of these women with half-grown children,
as I am any father
here with his grown daughter,

despite what you too knew, the steep
climb from minute to minute, day to day;
the insectile rush down across the mind;
and the various emptinesses, some rainbowy . . .

By your life- and
death-house I make my funny bow.
Then *with the word the time*, I'm quoting Shakespeare,
down toward Camden Town

where whole housefronts have been redone
as 60s bandit faces . . .
Effortful line, *the time will bring on summer*,
as if we had to help on

what happens anyway, *when briars shall
have leaves as well as thorns* (*All's Well*, the play
no one's quite easy with, because the characters
are allowed to be so bad before they're good.)

How long ago you taught me
knowledge that did not save you,
how near the insect footprints across the mind
are to its spaces of columnar blue.

Nostos

The story we all want told, and no one
wants to tell it. Or knows how.
To say what happens after things stop happening,
without despair or boredom—the hero archaic, reclining
by his wife on the couch—but no false fade-out, either;
for death is there, implied in the stilled inlet,
the bedpost rooted down in the dark earth.

The thing we're at home with is different from the many
things we can love: a fuller rhyme with childhood;
the poem of her life
legible to him, the light-hearted city, the cats,
the small creature-faces on her shelves; a quietness
that comes, even, from being peevish in the same way.

Yes, the goddesses were marvellous. The one
who'd been everywhere—the Kennedy compounds, the poppy fields
where she had to turn back, before the roof of everything;
and been, it seems, to the underside of the world,
from the things she knew about him before she knew him . . .
The one who painted circles with no horizon.

And the king's daughter: the hardest
to leave behind, the new dream of a human start.

But now it is time for home. Now
they lie and look out at the elements, water, light,
the pre-human near-touch of the mountains,
his hand along her arm towards the window,
and know their journey is the only one
anyone takes: farther into the body and its moments,
without a story; the journey all stories hide us from.

Perhaps it might feel like the making of the planet,
when the lava stopped taking every wildest form,
and mountains were mountains, streams were streams.
It would say that struggle needn't be felt as limit.
It would say the wandering lights were part of a warmth;
and when the lights were swallowed up in warmth,
how he didn't miss them, as he had, it seemed,
all his life long.

Notes

The Muse of Distance

"The Light's Reading": I have deliberately tried to make the boundaries between "meditation" and descriptions of paintings invisible in this poem. But the pictures recognizably present in it are, in this order: *Summertime, Second Story Sunlight, Summer in the City, Self-Portrait* (1945), *Two Comedians, Jo Painting.*

"The Prayer of the Cathars": All of the inset quotations in English come from a prayer or, more accurately, a credo of the Cathars, preserved in the records of the Inquisition, which I came across in France in a book of troubadour poetry (unfortunately, I have lost the reference). *Can vei la lauzeta mover* (*When I saw the skylark move*) by Bernart de Ventadorn is one of the most famous troubadour love poems. It is sung by Russell Oberlin on the record *Troubadour and Trouvère Songs* (*Expériences Anonymes*). I am indebted to many sources for this poem, but especially to Zoe Oldenbourg's remarkable and painful novel *Destiny of Fire*, and to Hugh Kenner's *The Pound Era.*

"*Art Roman*"—the French term for what we call "Romanesque"—means, literally, "Roman art." Moving from the Roman gate at Autun (which was, in fact, an *oppidum*, a frontier garrison-town) to the rounded arches of the cathedral, one can see why. The images at the end of the poem come from Chauvigny, near Poitiers. The art of Poitou-Charente (not, in fact, a "Cathar kingdom," but nearer to their part of France) has a metamorphic quality that contrasts sharply with the beauty and terror—the childlike men, the almost Pre-Raphaelite women, the tremendous Last Judgments—of the Burgundian churches.

"Recitation for the Dismantling of a Hydrogen Bomb": Any poem of this kind should, I think, be a collective as well as an individual undertaking. This one would not have taken the shape it did without the ABC-TV movie *The Day After*; Bach's *St. Matthew Passion*; Thomas J. J. Altizer and William Hamilton's *Radical Theology and*

· 247 ·

the Death of God; and Jonathan Schell's *The Fate of the Earth*. The work done in the Boston area in the late 1970s by Dr. Herbert Benson and Jon Kabat-Zinn on the use of meditation in the treatment of chronic pain offered a metaphor for what it could be like to survive, knowing that the means of collective self-destruction are always (conceptually) available.

Love and the Soul

"Love and the Soul": The lines in quotation marks are taken, with permission, from Louise Gluck's wonderful essay "The Dreamer and the Watcher." The "man whose wife / kept dead mice and owls in the refrigerator" was the critic R. P. Blackmur.

"Deb's Dream About Pavese": The italicized lines in the second stanza are taken, somewhat randomly, from Pavese's diaries (*This Business of Living*, Quartet Books, 1980).

"Unanticipated Mirrors": The "poet" is Juan Ramón Jiménez, "Dejad las puertas abiertas" (*The Penguin Book of Spanish Verse*, p. 425). The "more poets," roughly paraphrased, are Shelley ("Adonais") and Hart Crane ("The Broken Tower").

"Tidepools": "Steinbeck's 'tidepool Johnnie' " is from *Cannery Row*, Chapter VI.

Res Publica

"Dreams of Sacrifice": cf. Alan Williamson, "Two Faces," *Poetry Northwest,* Autumn 1972.

"Listening to Leonard Cohen": "In the dawn of time": cf. Wordsworth, *The Prelude,* Book XI, ll. 108–9. I did live through the end of the 1960s in Charlottesville, Virginia. "Beulah" and "Ulro" are Blakean terms: Beulah, roughly, the Earthly Paradise we discover when the imagination invests itself in the external world and the external world reveals hidden depths; Ulro, the Hell we fall into when we live by unexamined imaginative premises, believing we live only by materialistic pragmatism. Blake was much in the minds of many people, particularly many academics, drawn to the counterculture, as a precedent for our way of thinking within the received canon. "*There is a grain of sand*": Blake, *Jerusalem,* Plate 37, ll. 15–19, Plate 35, ll. 1–2. "*heroes in the seaweed*," etc.: cf. Leonard Cohen, "Suzanne." "*Oh Lord*": Janis Joplin, "Mercedes Benz." "*I saw a beggar*": Leonard Cohen, "Bird on a Wire." The "Jesus freaks," as we called them, did actually picket a lecture by R. D. Laing in Charlottesville, with the leaflet described.

"Speakers from the Ice": cf. *Inferno,* XXXIII–XXXIV. The poem also owes a debt to Molly Giles's great story "Talking to Strangers."

"*La Pastorela*": a Hispanic Christmas play, performed every other year at the Mission in San Juan Bautista by the Teatro Campesino, a group which had its origins in Cesar Chavez's United Farm Workers movement. A few years ago there was a televised version, with an elaborate frame-story (retold, in part, in the poem), and with Linda Ronstadt as the Archangel Michael. The stories referred to in 1.6, and in the next-to-last stanza, were much in the news in 1992 and 1993.

"Mansard Dreams": "Einstein": cf. Jon Kabat-Zinn, *Full Catastrophe Living* (New York: Delta, 1990), p. 165. "Dogen": "The Time-Being," *Moon in a Dewdrop* (Berkeley, CA: North Point Press, 1985).

"Puccini Dying": Puccini did stop writing *Turandot* more or less at the point where Timur follows Liu's corpse offstage; the concluding love duet was completed, from his notes, by Alfano. The Doria story, and the story of his late trip to Florence to hear Schoenberg, can be found in Mosco Carner's *Puccini* (New York: Knopf, 1959).

"*In Paradiso, speriamo bene*": "It's in his biography": cf. Paul Mariani, *Lost Puritan* (New York: W.W. Norton, 1994), pp. 379–80. "Gorgeous as a jungle bird": Lowell, "Beyond the Alps."

"Caitlin: A Biography": "Crying *What I do*": Gerard Manley Hopkins, "As Kingfishers Catch Fire."

"Red Cloud": All quotes come either from Willa Cather, *The Song of the Lark,* or from James Woodress's *Willa Cather: A Literary Life* (Lincoln: University of Nebraska Press, 1987), or Sharon O'Brien's *Willa Cather: The Emerging Voice* (New York: Oxford University Press, 1987). Three bows: a Zen observance, lifting the feet of Buddha over one's head.

New Poems: The Pattern More Complicated

"A Place": cf. *Inferno*, I, ll. 16–18:
guardai in alto e vidi le sue spalle
vestite già de' raggi del pianeta
che mena dritto altrui per ogni calle.

"Fantasia on some sentences from *Combray*": The Proust quotes come from *Swann's Way*, tr. C. K. Scott Moncrieff and Terence Kilmartin, rev. D. J. Enright (London: Vintage, 1996), pp. 201, 205, 221. Eliot: "Little Gidding," III, ll. 10–11.

"Primrose Hill": I am probably one of the few writers—or at least the few male writers—to regard Sylvia Plath as not only a technical but a spiritual teacher. Primrose Hill is the neighborhood in London where she spent the last two months of her life. *All's Well*: IV, iv, ll. 31–33.

"Nostos": the name given in Greek to the last books of the *Odyssey*, in which Odysseus returns home, kills the suitors, and is reunited with Penelope; thus, the archetypal instance of a successful happy ending.